International Trade and Core Labour Standards

OECD 《●

ORGANISATION FOR ECONOMIC CO-OPERATION AND DEVELOPMENT

ORGANISATION FOR ECONOMIC CO-OPERATION AND DEVELOPMENT

Pursuant to Article 1 of the Convention signed in Paris on 14th December 1960, and which came into force on 30th September 1961, the Organisation for Economic Co-operation and Development (OECD) shall promote policies designed:

- to achieve the highest sustainable economic growth and employment and a rising standard of living in Member countries, while maintaining financial stability, and thus to contribute to the development of the world economy;

- to contribute to sound economic expansion in Member as well as non-member countries in the process of economic development; and

- to contribute to the expansion of world trade on a multilateral, non-discriminatory basis in accordance with international obligations.

The original Member countries of the OECD are Austria, Belgium, Canada, Denmark, France, Germany, Greece, Iceland, Ireland, Italy, Luxembourg, the Netherlands, Norway, Portugal, Spain, Sweden, Switzerland, Turkey, the United Kingdom and the United States. The following countries became Members subsequently through accession at the dates indicated hereafter: Japan (28th April 1964), Finland (28th January 1969), Australia (7th June 1971), New Zealand (29th May 1973), Mexico (18th May 1994), the Czech Republic (21st December 1995), Hungary (7th May 1996), Poland (22nd November 1996) and Korea (12th December 1996). The Commission of the European Communities takes part in the work of the OECD (Article 13 of the OECD Convention).

Publié en français sous le titre :
LES ÉCHANGES INTERNATIONAUX ET LES NORMES FONDAMENTALES DU TRAVAIL

Foreword

In 1996, the OECD published a study entitled *Trade, Employment and Labour Standards: A Study of Core Workers' Rights and International Trade*, which responded to a request from OECD Ministers for analysis of areas where further progress with liberalisation and strengthening of the multilateral system may be required. The study was instrumental in helping foster a high degree of international political consensus about the definition of a limited set of core labour standards.

Since the 1996 study was completed there have been a number of significant developments with respect to core labour standards. Two important milestones were the inclusion of a statement on core labour standards in the Declaration issued at the First WTO Ministerial Meeting in Singapore in December 1996 and the adoption in June 1998 of the ILO Declaration on Fundamental Principles and Rights at Work. This report analyses those and other developments that have occurred since 1996. It also includes a review of the economic literature published since then. While in this respect the present report can be seen as a companion piece to the 1996 study, it is also intended to be a stand-alone publication in its own right.

International Trade and Core Labour Standards has benefited from extensive discussion within the OECD Committees which oversaw this work, the Trade Committee and the Employment, Labour and Social Affairs Committee, as well as from comments received from the International Labour Office and two advisory committees to the OECD, the Business and Industry Advisory Committee and the Trade Union Advisory Committee.

It has emerged from this latest work that the major findings of the earlier study remain largely valid. At the same time, certain aspects of the complex interplay between trade, employment and core labour standards continue to attract differing views, including among OECD Member countries. The object of this report is therefore to seek to widen the area of common ground on one of the most sensitive issues of the ongoing policy dialogue about globalisation and the intensification of international trade and investment.

The report was drafted by a team from the Secretariat composed of Dale Andrew and Douglas Lippoldt, with inputs provided by Kathryn Gordon, Frans Lammersen and Carole Pellegrino. The team worked under the supervision of Ken Heydon and John P. Martin. The report is published on the responsibility of the Secretary-General.

Table of Contents

List of Boxes

List of Tables

List of Charts

Abbreviations

ACP	African, Caribbean and Pacific Countries (associated with EU)
ADB	Asian Development Bank
AfDB	African Development Bank
AFL-CIO	American Federation of Labor and Congress of Industrial Organizations
CAS	Country Assistance Strategies (World Bank)
CEACR	Committee of Experts on the Application of Conventions and Recommendations (ILO)
CEC	*Confédération Européenne de la Chaussure (European Confederation of the Footwear Industry)*
CEDC	Programme on Children in Especially Difficult Circumstances (UNICEF)
CEDDEC	European Confederation of the Shoe Retail Association
CFA	Committee on Freedom of Association (ILO)
CIME	Committee on International Investment and Multinational Enterprises (OECD)
COTANCE	Confederation of National Associations of Tanners and Dressers of the European Community
DAC	Development Assistance Committee (OECD)
DIP	Double Income Project
EC	European Community
EPZ	Export-processing zone
ETI	Ethical Trading Initiative
ETUC	European Trade Union Confederation
ETUF:TCL	European Trade Union Federation of Textiles, Clothing and Leather
EU	European Union
EURATEX	European Apparel and Textile Organisation
FDI	Foreign direct investment
FIET	International Federation of Commercial, Clerical, Professional and Technical Employees.
FLO	Fairtrade Labelling Organisation
GATT	General Agreement on Tariffs and Trade
GDP	Gross domestic product
GSP	Generalised System of Preferences
ICFTU	International Confederation of Free Trade Unions
IDB	Inter-american Development Bank Group
IEPCE	Initiative for Ethical Consumption and Production in Europe
IFBWW	International Federation of Building and Wood Workers

ILO	International Labour Organisation
IMF	International Monetary Fund
IPEC	International Programme on the Elimination of Child Labour (ILO)
MERCOSUR	*Mercado Commún del Sur* (Common Market of the Southern Cone)
MFN	Most-favoured nation
MNE	Multinational enterprise
MoU	Memorandum of understanding
NAALC	North American Agreement on Labor Cooperation
NAFTA	North American Free Trade Agreement
NAO	National Administrative Office
NBER	National Bureau for Economic Research
NGO	Non-governmental organisation
QRs	Quantitative restrictions
SADC	Southern African Development Community
SRI	Socially responsible investing
TPRB	Trade Policy Review Body (WTO)
TUAC	Trade Union Advisory Committee to the OECD
UN	United Nations
UNCTAD	United Nations Conference on Trade and Development
UNESCO	United Nations Educational, Scientific and Cultural Organisation
UNICEF	United Nations International Children's Emergency Fund
USITC	United States International Trade Commission
USTR	US Trade Representative
WTO	World Trade Organisation

Overview

Factual developments since completion of the 1996 study

Since the 1996 OECD study was completed, there have been wide-ranging developments, at the national and international levels, bearing on the question of trade, employment and core labour standards. These are summarised below.

There is now a high degree of international political consensus on the contents of a set of core labour standards

The international community has made significant progress in developing a consensus with respect to the definition and recognition of a small set of core labour standards.

That consensus has been given international recognition by strengthened ILO provisions

A key milestone came in June 1998 with the adoption of the ILO Declaration on Fundamental Principles and Rights at Work, which succinctly stated four principles, committed the ILO's member states to respect them and stressed that labour standards are not to be used for protectionist trade purposes.

In recalling the importance of the ILO's fundamental conventions, the ILO Declaration extended the range of reporting on the application of the fundamental principles and rights to include countries that have not ratified fundamental conventions.

In June 1999, the ILO members adopted a new fundamental convention (No. 182) banning the *worst forms* of child labour. With its entry into force in November 2000, it is set to become the eighth fundamental convention.

And commitment to those provisions has increased

Since October 1995, the number of countries that have ratified all seven of the original fundamental conventions has more than doubled. The new fundamental convention on the worst forms of child labour has experienced a rapid pace of ratification.

Though more needs to be done, especially on the enforcement front

Although the country coverage of ratifications is extensive, follow-up is still required to improve monitoring and to include non-ratifying countries. And – although there has been some improvement – there remain substantial gaps between the ratification of the fundamental conventions and the application of principles in practice.

Based on published observations of the ILO Committee of Experts on the Application of Conventions and Recommendations, there is no clear indication of substantial progress overall in reducing non-compliance with respect to freedom of association and the right to collective bargaining among a broad sample of countries that have ratified the corresponding ILO conventions.

In the meantime, the ILO has introduced a new promotional mechanism and strengthened its technical co-operation

The 1998 ILO Declaration established a follow-up mechanism to promote the fundamental principles and rights at work, including a special annual report designed to provide a dynamic global picture of the situation and facilitate the assessment and prioritisation of ILO technical co-operation activities. Through this mechanism and other initiatives, the ILO is giving renewed impetus to its already substantial technical co -operation efforts. While it will take time before the full effects of these changes are known, it appears that some countries are responsive to the increased international scrutiny and assistance.

A future challenge will be to find a way for the system to focus international attention on the most serious shortcomings in a way that leads to early improvements, while maintaining efforts to promote increased respect for labour standards in the law and practice of Member countries in general.

The trade and labour issue continues to be debated in the WTO

At Singapore in December 1996, WTO members renewed their commitment to the observance of internationally recognised core labour standards, supported collaboration between the WTO and ILO Secretariats, rejected the use of labour standards for protectionist purposes and recognised that the ILO is the competent body to set and deal with core labour standards.

At the Third WTO Ministerial meeting at Seattle, in December 1999, the US proposed a WTO Working Group on Trade and Labour, the EU a joint ILO/WTO Standing Working Forum on the issue, and Canada a WTO Working Group on the relationships between appropriate trade, developmental, social and environmental policy choices in the context of adjusting to globalisation. These proposals were opposed by a number of WTO Members.

Regional and unilateral government actions have continued to provide incentives for the promotion and implementation of core standards

Efforts have continued within the North American Agreement on Labor Cooperation to resolve labour law issues by promoting enforcement of existing labour laws in the three Member countries.

Two regional economic integration agreements – Mercosur and SADC (Southern African Development Community) – have both recently advanced towards adoption of social charters endorsing a series of labour principles and providing for monitoring of implementation.

Under the US GSP scheme, benefits were suspended in a case involving bonded child labour and failure to allow for freedom of association. And country practice reviews are used to obtain improvements in worker rights in certain countries.

Under the EC GSP scheme, the main focus is the provision of additional trade preferences to countries that can demonstrate their compliance with certain core labour standards. The EC GSP scheme also allows for temporary suspension of preferences, to be decided under certain circumstances.

The US has passed legislation prohibiting the manufacture or import of goods produced by forced or indentured child labour.

The US has negotiated a statement of co-operation with a major exporter of labour-intensive goods allowing US embassy officials to visit prisons suspected of operating factories with goods for export.

Commitments to core labour standards were also included in a partnership agreement between the European

Community and the ACP countries and a trade, development and co-operation agreement between the European Community and South Africa.

There has been a strengthened commitment through development co-operation to eradicate exploitative forms of child labour

The contribution of development co-operation programmes in eradicating exploitative forms of child labour has become more focussed and result-oriented.

The DAC Strategy (1996) "Shaping the 21st Century: The Contribution of Development Co-operation" commits donors to assist partners in achieving universal access to primary education in all countries by 2015.

Core labour standards and their operational implications have taken on heightened importance for the World Bank, within its mandate on poverty reduction and economic and social development, and for many other international financial institutions.

Guidelines, codes of conduct and private-party mechanisms have also gained wider scope and coverage

Efforts are also continuing to harness international investment and multinational enterprises to promote core labour standards worldwide. For example, a comprehensive review of the OECD Guidelines for Multinational Enterprises was completed in June 2000.

The Review aimed to ensure the continued relevance and effectiveness of the Guidelines. It added recommendations in relation to those core labour standards that were missing from the earlier text (child labour and forced labour, in particular). The revised recommendations make it clear that they apply to enterprises operating in or from adhering countries and that they are relevant for their operations in all countries. The Guidelines are part of a broad and balanced package of instruments, under the OECD Declaration on International Investment and Multinational Enterprise, designed to further international co-operation in the field of international investment and multinational enterprise.

Voluntary codes of conduct – written expressions of commitment to a given standard of business conduct – have continued to grow in number. For example, in the US, most Fortune 500 companies have adopted codes of conduct or internal guidelines, dealing with a variety of matters, including core labour standards. In the UK, over 60% of the top 500 companies have similar codes; a decade ago the figure was only 18%. The social partners from the textiles and clothing, footwear and commerce sectors in the EU have negotiated codes of conduct based on core labour standards.

The incidence of moral suasion and labelling appears to have increased since the 1996 study was completed.

Export-processing zones – sometimes outside national labour laws – have grown in number

EPZs, outside China, have grown from some 500 at the time of the 1996 study to about 850, employing 27 million people. In addition, there are several hundred EPZs operating in China.

In some countries national labour legislation does not apply to EPZs. And the ILO concludes that problematic factors such as high labour turnover, absenteeism, stress and fatigue, low rates of productivity, excessive wastage of materials and labour unrest are still too common in zones. At the same time, wages in EPZs tend to be higher than average wages in the rest of the economy.

But investors, including in EPZs, increasingly seek investment locations with highly skilled workers

Increasing international competition is changing the priorities for foreign investors who tend to favour investment locations with highly skilled workers and modern infrastructure. "Smart" EPZs have adopted strategies to ensure that labour productivity is continuously upgraded.

More broadly, recent FDI data confirm that MNEs invest principally in the largest, richest and most dynamic markets. With the notable exception of China, countries where core labour standards are not respected continue to receive a very small share of global investment flows. There is no robust evidence that low-standard countries provide a haven for foreign firms.

Conclusions from the literature review

A search of relevant literature in the public domain, since the 1996 study was completed, enables a number of tentative conclusions to be drawn. While some important principles remain valid, the literature review highlights that caution is needed in seeking to interpret the complex interplay between trade, employment and labour standards.

Strengthened core labour standards can increase economic growth and efficiency

Countries which strengthen their core labour standards can increase economic efficiency by raising skill levels in the workforce and by creating an environment which encourages innovation and higher productivity.

And high standards may ease the adjustment arising from trade liberalisation

Some recent studies consider the links between trade, democracy and wages. The results suggest that countries that develop democratic institutions – here taken to include core labour rights – before the transition to trade liberalisation will weather the transition with smaller adverse consequences than countries without such institutions.

Countries with low core labour standards do not enjoy better export performance than high-standard countries

Recent studies suggesting a negative relationship between observance of labour standards and trade performance do not challenge the finding of the 1996 study that countries with low core labour standards do not enjoy better export performance than high-standard countries because these recent studies focus on labour standards generally and not on core labour standards. This distinction is crucial for analytical purposes because core and non-core labour standards are expected to have different, and often opposite, effects on economic outcomes.

Opinions continue to differ about the impact of trade on employment patterns and/or wage inequality

There continues to be disagreement among researchers on the size of the trade impact on sectoral employment patterns and/or wage inequality relative to the impact of other forces, *e.g.* technological progress, international migration and institutional change.

Many studies confirm a role for trade, but the contribution is limited. Moreover, the fact that relative wage inequality has risen in some developing countries (as well as in some OECD countries) poses a problem for standard trade theory. Had trade been the driver, the Stolper-Samuelson theorem would have led one to expect that developing countries, exporting unskilled labour-intensive goods, would have experienced a convergence in the relative wage of skilled and unskilled workers rather than growing inequality.

Fears about a "race to the bottom" in labour standards are probably exaggerated

A number of recent studies point out that there are major constraints on a "race to the bottom" in labour standards. Any firm that attempts to gain a competitive advantage by cutting benefits without paying increased money wages is essentially trying to cut wages below the workers' marginal value product. In competitive markets, pressure from other employers will ultimately force the firm to return the total compensation package to the original level if the firm expects to be able to hire workers. But where such competitive pressures are weak the outcome may be different. Often there are costs to search, to finding out what wages other firms are offering, and even greater costs associated with moving from one employer to another. However, again it should be recalled that insofar as discussion of a "race to the bottom" focuses on wage levels it is not relevant to the question of core labour standards.

In some circumstances a ban on child labour may be effective

Some recent literature suggests that governments of countries in which children are employed may choose to change their laws rather than bear the cost of trade sanctions. It is also suggested that, in certain circumstances, a ban on child labour may be effective in shifting the economy into an equilibrium where adult wages are high and children do not work. This could apply to countries with relatively high labour productivity that are able to support all their children without sending any to work.

Though there are practical limits to such a policy

However, the literature also suggests that, in very poor countries, a ban may worsen the condition of households. Moreover, a ban on the import of goods which have used child labour as an input might drive child labour out of export industries but is likely to do little to prevent child labour in the informal sector which is the major employer of child workers in such countries.

And better policies than trade interventions are available

Recent analysis, drawing on experience in Brazil and Mexico, suggests that a subsidy to families to keep their children in school is likely to be a superior policy to, for example, trade interventions, in terms of curbing child labour. Trade interventions are not an optimal instrument to abolish exploitative child labour and expand human capital formation.

15

Part I

Labour Standards in OECD and Selected Non-OECD Countries

The 1996 OECD study defined labour standards as "norms and rules that govern working conditions and industrial relations" [OECD (1996*b*, p. 25)]. While labour standards exist concerning a broad range of labour market issues, there is no single set of standards with universal coverage in terms of content or geography. Labour standards with force of law may be established by national governments or international bodies such as the European Union. However, the most widely accepted standards are embodied in the ILO conventions and several UN acts (see Box 1). These international treaties have a binding "character" for those countries that ratify them, but they are not enforced through sanctions.[1]

The international community has confirmed the primacy of the ILO among international organisations with respect to key aspects of labour standards. An important milestone in this regard was the Singapore Ministerial Conference of the WTO in December 1996 (with more than 120 nations participating). A declaration issued at that conference: *i*) highlighted the commitment of the participating nations to observe internationally-recognised core labour standards; *ii*) affirmed the ILO as "the competent body to set and deal with these standards"; *iii*) restated support for the ILO in promoting the standards; *iv*) rejected the use of labour standards for protectionist purposes; and *v*) confirmed that the WTO and ILO secretariats would continue their existing collaboration [WTO (1996)].

Core labour standards and the ILO Declaration on Fundamental Principles and Rights at Work

"Core" labour standards are accorded particular importance internationally because they reflect basic human rights in the workplace, provide for framework conditions that facilitate the meaningful application of other labour standards, and promote the expression of free choice that is a key element in the healthy functioning of market economies. In the period since the OECD's 1996 study, a high degree of international political consensus has developed with respect to the

---

Box 1. Selected United Nations Acts

The 1996 study highlighted the important role of the UN in the promotion of human rights, including workers' rights. Promotion and respect for human rights and basic liberties are among the obligations of membership laid down in the charter of the UN, and spelt out in more detail in the Universal Declaration of Human Rights of 1948. Among the UN acts, the 1996 study cited three of particular relevance to core labour standards:

- the Covenant on Economic, Social and Cultural Rights of 1966 (which cites rights at work concerning equal opportunity in employment and freedom of association and trade union functioning, among others);
- the Covenant on Civil and Political Rights of 1966 (which cites such rights at work as freedom of association, prohibition of forced labour and equality before the law, among others); and
- the Convention on the Rights of the Child (adopted in 1989) (which establishes the principle of non-exploitation of child labour and certain related rights).

While the various provisions in these UN acts are similar to the ILO conventions, they tend to be less detailed. In some cases, the UN acts are more broadly accepted than the ILO conventions (*e.g.*, with respect to child labour) or have different country coverage in terms of ratifications. As a result, the UN acts help to complement and complete the protection of labour standards afforded under international law. This may, in part, be the result of additional flexibility in the UN procedures which permit countries to ratify acts while declaring reservations.

Table 1 highlights the ratifications of the three UN acts. In each case, there has been a significant increase in the number of ratifications since end-1994. The UN Convention on the Rights of the Child has near-universal acceptance, while the other two acts have about the same number of ratifications as most ILO fundamental conventions. Also, the number of countries ratifying all three UN acts is more than twice as large as the number ratifying all ILO fundamental conventions.

---

definition of a set of core labour standards. These standards are reflected in the list of fundamental principles and rights laid out in the ILO *Declaration on Fundamental Principles and Rights at Work* (hereafter, "ILO Declaration", [ILO (1998*a*)]). According to the ILO Declaration, these principles and rights include:

a) freedom of association and the effective recognition of the right to collective bargaining;

b) the elimination of all forms of forced or compulsory labour;

c) the effective abolition of child labour; and

d) the elimination of discrimination in respect of employment and occupation.

The extent of the consensus is exemplified by the support for the ILO Declaration, which was adopted at the June 1998 International Labour Conference with no opposing votes.[2]

The ILO Declaration notes that the fundamental principles and rights have been "expressed and developed in the form of specific rights and obligations" laid out in the ILO's fundamental conventions. Thus, for those countries that have ratified them, the fundamental conventions constitute an important application of the four fundamental principles and rights. The list of fundamental conventions is not defined in the Declaration itself, but rather is determined by the ILO's Governing Body. (The correspondence between the fundamental principles and rights at work and the fundamental conventions is shown in Box 2). According to the Declaration,

"all Members, even if they have not ratified the Conventions in question, have an obligation, arising from the very fact of membership in the Organisation to respect, to promote and to realise, in good faith and in accordance with the Constitution, the principles concerning the fundamental rights which are the subject of those Conventions…".

Thus, while the decisions to join the ILO or to ratify a given convention remain the sovereign right of each ILO Member, membership also brings certain obligations with respect to the fundamental principles and rights that are reflected in the fundamental conventions. At the same time, the ILO Declaration affirms the point made at the Singapore WTO Ministerial that labour standards should not be used for protectionist trade purposes.

Seen from an international legal perspective, the ILO Declaration is less formal than the ILO conventions and recommendations that form the basis of the ILO's system of international labour standards. The ILO Declaration is rather an affirmation of fundamental principles and rights, with an important promotional dimension. Through this document, the ILO members restated the organisation's obligation to assist members with implementation of the fundamental principles (*e.g.*, by providing technical co-operation) and instituted follow-up based on a reporting mechanism with two components: *i*) annual reports from countries that have not ratified a given fundamental convention; and *ii*) a global report covering all ILO members that each year will provide a dynamic picture of the situation with respect to one of the four categories of fundamental principles and rights, assessing the ILO's assistance efforts and outlining priorities for future technical co-operation.[3]

In defining the fundamental principles and rights, the ILO Declaration drew on the conclusions of the March 1995 World Summit on Social Development held in Copenhagen. The Programme of Action agreed at the Summit committed the participants to safeguard and promote "basic workers' rights" and listed these using a formulation similar to the one later incorporated into the ILO Declaration.[4]

19

Box 2. **The fundamental principles and rights at work
and the fundamental conventions, as laid out in ILO documents
and decisions**

1. **Freedom of association and the effective recognition of the right to collective bargaining**

   - Freedom of Association and Protection of the Right to Organise Convention, 1948 (No. 87).
   - Right to Organise and Collective Bargaining Convention, 1949 (No. 98).

2. **Elimination of all forms of forced or compulsory labour**

   - Forced Labour Convention, 1930 (No. 29).
   - Abolition of Forced Labour Convention, 1957 (No. 105).

3. **Effective abolition of child labour**

   - Minimum Age Convention, 1973 (No. 138).
   - Worst Forms of Child Labour Convention, 1999 (No. 182) [This convention is now designated as the eighth fundamental convention (effective upon its entry into force on 19 November 2000)].*

4. **Elimination of discrimination in respect of employment and occupation**

   - Equal Remuneration Convention, 1951 (No. 100).
   - Discrimination (Employment and Occupation) Convention, 1958 (No. 111).

   ---

   * Conventions are not binding on ratifying states until they have formally entered into force. Normally, this first occurs 12 months after registration of ratifications by two ILO Member countries. Thereafter, entries into force occur on an individual basis for each ratifying country 12 months after registration of its ratification [ILO (1999a)]. The ratification of Convention No. 182 by the Seychelles (in September 1999) and Malawi (in November 1999) started the countdown for its entry into force.

The OECD's 1996 study also defined core labour standards in a similar fashion, but focused on a group of five core conventions (No. 29, 87, 98, 105 and 111) rather than the ILO's original seven fundamental conventions.[5] The Equal Remuneration Convention (No. 100) was not considered separately because the principles it represents were viewed as being embodied in Convention 111 on non-discrimination. A second exception concerned the abolition of child labour. The OECD study noted that in many countries part-time work by children is "a fact of life" and "not necessarily exploitative or detrimental to the child's development". Therefore, a further qualification was added targeting "elimination of *exploitative* forms of child labour, such as bonded labour and forms of child labour that put the health and safety of children at serious risk". At the time of the 1996 study and, indeed, at the time of the 1998 ILO Declaration, no ILO convention targeted these issues specifically with respect to children.

Until recently, the main ILO protections against abuse of children at work were provided under Convention 29 that calls for the suppression and abolition of forced labour and under Convention 138 that provides for a minimum age of employment (generally taken to be 15 years of age or older).[6] With the unanimous adoption of the Worst Forms of Child Labour Convention (No. 182) at the ILO's June 1999 Conference, a new protection was added that specifically bans with respect to children all forms of slavery or practices similar to slavery, forced or compulsory labour, sexual exploitation, illicit activities and work likely to harm the health, safety or morals of children.

Progress in ratification of the ILO's fundamental conventions

Ratification of any ILO convention is generally intended to reflect a member state's acceptance of the convention without reservations, commitment to apply it in practice, and agreement to submit to ILO supervision of its implementation.[7] There are a variety of reasons for non-ratification, including instances where countries agree in principle with a convention but cannot accept its provisions without reservation. This is sometimes due to peculiarities in a country's domestic law or practice. For example, in some countries with a federal form of government such as Switzerland or the United States, the devolution of authority may limit the ability of the national government to make binding commitments on constituent entities (*e.g.*, cantons and states). In other instances, countries object due to particular interpretations of conventions by ILO bodies, issues of international law or other legal reasons.

In recent years, the ILO has pressed its Member countries for ratification of the fundamental conventions. A campaign to this effect was launched in May 1995 following the ILO's 75th Anniversary and the World Summit on Social Development in Copenhagen. Since then, each year the ILO secretariat reports to the ILO Governing Body on progress and prospects for ratification of these conventions and on related technical assistance. These ratification efforts were endorsed through the ILO Declaration. Also, when the new convention against the Worst Forms of Child Labour was adopted, the ILO launched a special campaign specifically promoting its ratification.

In the years since the 1996 study, the ILO campaign has borne fruit (see Table 1); the increase in ratifications is considerable. Since October 1995, the number of ILO Member states ratifying all of the original fundamental

21

Table 1. **Progress in ratifications of selected ILO and UN conventions and covenants**

	OECD 1996 Study		OECD 2000 Update		
	All countries	OECD countries (25 total)	All countries	OECD countries (29 total)[a]	Of the 76 countries in the 2000 report
ILO fundamental conventions[b]	As of October 1995		As of June 2000		
ILO Convention No. 29 (forced labour)	137	22	153	26	69
ILO Convention No. 87 (freedom of association)	113	23	130	26	59
ILO Convention No. 98 (right to organise and collective bargaining)	125	20	146	24	66
ILO Convention No. 100 (equal remuneration)[c]	126	24	147	28	66
ILO Convention No. 105 (abolition of forced labour)	115	24	145	27	70
ILO Convention No. 111 (non-discrimination in employment and occupation)	119	20	143	26	63
ILO Convention No. 138 (minimum age)[c]	49	12	93	22	49
Number of countries that ratified all ILO conventions listed above[d]	27	10	63	19	34
UN Convention and Covenants	As of end 1994		As of October 1999		
UN Covenant on Civil and Political Rights	129	23	145	28	64
UN Covenant on Economic, Social and Cultural Rights	131	23	142	27	62
UN Convention on the Rights of the Child	168	21	187	28	75
Number of countries that have ratified all UN acts listed above[e]	123	20	138	27	61

a) Four new Member countries joined the OECD after October 1995: the Czech Republic, Hungary, Korea and Poland.
b) The original seven ILO fundamental conventions [i.e., prior to the entry into force of the eighth fundamental convention – the Worst Forms of Child Labour Convention (No. 182)].
c) Conventions 100 and 138 were not included in the original version of this table in the 1996 study.
d) As of June 2000, there were 175 ILO Member states.
e) As of October 1999, there were 189 UN Member countries.
Sources: ILO (1999b), ILO (1999e), UN (1999) and OECD (1996b).

conventions has more than doubled. The number of OECD countries doing so increased by nine. Except for Korea and the United States, all OECD countries have ratified four or more of the fundamental conventions. Also, in the year following its adoption, the Worst Forms of Child Labour Convention received 27 ratifications, more than any previous convention during a comparable period. While the fundamental conventions have not yet received universal ratification, the principles that they represent have come to represent obligations associated with membership in the ILO. Nevertheless, it is noteworthy that as of June 2000 only just over a third of the ILO Member countries have ratified all the original fundamental conventions (including 19 OECD countries).

Observance of core labour standards in selected countries

Core labour standards are reflected in the ILO fundamental principles and rights and, in turn, those principles and rights are "expressed and developed" in the ILO fundamental conventions. This section reviews the situation of those fundamental conventions in the 76 countries covered by the OECD's 1996 study.[8] These countries include OECD countries, so-called dynamic non-member economies (*i.e.*, Argentina, Brazil, Chile, Chinese Taipei, Hong Kong, China,[9] Malaysia, the Philippines, Singapore and Thailand), as well as three populous countries with considerable trade potential (China, India and Indonesia) and a range of poor countries throughout the world for which information could be collected. Taken together, the countries covered in this section account for the vast majority of world trade.

Annex Table A.1 presents basic economic indicators for these countries. Per capita GDP levels (in 1995) ranged from US$98 in Ethiopia to US$42 719 in Switzerland. As expected, per capita GDP is on average highest in the OECD area. However, in a number of non-OECD countries, per capita GDP is higher than in Poland and Turkey, the two lowest-income OECD economies. For example, Hong Kong, China and Singapore are somewhat above the OECD average, while Israel and Kuwait have levels of per capita GDP amounting to about three-quarters of the OECD average (well above the lowest quintile of OECD countries).

Table 2 provides information on the progress in ratifications of the fundamental conventions by the 76 countries in question. The progress in ratifications summarised in Table 1 above is clearly seen in Table 2. Over 40% of the countries in Table 2 have ratified all seven original fundamental conventions. Several countries significantly increased their ratification record: Botswana, Chile, Indonesia, South Africa and Zimbabwe each newly ratified four or more of the conventions. At the other extreme, as of June 2000, China and Singapore had each ratified a total of only two of the fundamental conventions and the United States only one.[10] Among the countries currently with the fewest ratifications of the original fundamental conventions, only China added a new ratification during the period since the 1996 study.

Among the fundamental principles and rights, the ILO gives particular emphasis to the freedom of association and right to collective bargaining. These are cited in the ILO Constitution and the Declaration of Philadelphia (1944), supervised through a special mechanism (described in detail in the OECD's 1996 study), and reflected in ILO Conventions 87 and 98.

Annex Tables A.2, A.3 and A.4 highlight changes and new information concerning countries' application of key elements of these conventions in the years since the 1996 study. Only observed developments are included; pending or planned actions are excluded. The table entries are based primarily on formal,

Table 2. **Ratification of ILO fundamental conventions, situation as of June 2000**[d]

(Bold print indicates ratifications since October 1995)

	Forced labour (Conv. 29)	Freedom of association (Conv. 87)	Right to organise and collective bargaining (Conv. 98)	Equal Remuneration (Conv. 100)[b]	Abolition of forced labour (Conv. 105)	Non-discrimination (Conv. 111)	Minimum Age (Conv. 138)[b]
Non-OECD							
Argentina	r	r	r	r	r	r	**R**
Bahamas	r		r		r		
Bangladesh	r	r	r	**R**	r	r	
Barbados	r	r	r	r	r	r	**R**
Bolivia		r	r	r	r	r	**R**
Botswana	**R**	**R**	**R**	**R**	**R**	**R**	**R**
Brazil	r		r	r	r	r	
Chile	r	**R**	**R**	r	**R**	r	**R**
China				r			**R**
Colombia	r	r	r	r	r	r	
Ecuador	r	r	r	r	r	r	
Egypt	r	r	r	r	r	r	**R**
Ethiopia		r	r	**R**	**R**	r	**R**
Fiji	r		r		r		
Guatemala	r	r	r	r	r	r	r
Haiti	r	r	r	r	r	r	
Honduras	r	r	r	r	r	r	r
Hong Kong, China	c	c	c		c		c
India	r			r	**R**	r	
Indonesia	r	**R**	r	r	**R**	**R**	**R**
Iran	r			r	r	r	
Israel	r	r	r	r	r	r	r
Jamaica	r	r	r	r	r	r	
Jordan	r		r	r	r	r	**R**
Kenya	r		r		r		**R**
Kuwait	r	r			r	r	**R**
Malaysia[d]	r		r	**R**			**R**
Malta	r	r	r	r	r	r	r
Mauritius	r		r		r		r
Morocco	r		r	r	r	r	**R**
Niger	r	r	r	r	r	r	r
Pakistan	r	r	r		r	r	
Panama	r	r	r	r	r	r	
Papua New Guinea	r	**R**	r	**R**	r	**R**	
Peru	r	r	r	r	r	r	
Philippines		r	r	r	r	r	**R**
Singapore[d]	r		r				
South Africa	**R**	**R**	**R**	**R**	**R**	**R**	**R**

Table 2. **Ratification of ILO fundamental conventions, situation as of June 2000^a** (*cont.*)

(Bold print indicates ratifications since October 1995)

	Forced labour (Conv. 29)	Freedom of association (Conv. 87)	Right to organise and collective bargaining (Conv. 98)	Equal Remuneration (Conv. 100)^b	Abolition of forced labour (Conv. 105)	Non-discrimination (Conv. 111)	Minimum Age (Conv. 138)^b
Sri Lanka	r	**R**	r	r		**R**	
Suriname	r	r	**R**		r		
Swaziland	r	r	r	r	r	r	
Syria	r	r	r	r	r	r	
Tanzania	r	**R**	r		r		**R**
Thailand	r			**R**	r		
Uruguay	**R**	r	r	r	r	r	r
Venezuela	r	r	r	r	r	r	r
Zambia	r	**R**	**R**	r	r	r	r
Zimbabwe	**R**		**R**	r	**R**	**R**	**R**
OECD							
Australia	r	r	r	r	r	r	
Austria	r	r	r	r	r	r	
Belgium	r	r	r	r	r	r	r
Canada		r		r	r	r	
Czech Republic	r	r	r	r	**R**	r	
Denmark	r	r	r	r	r	r	**R**
Finland	r	r	r	r	r	r	r
France	r	r	r	r	r	r	r
Germany	r	r	r	r	r	r	r
Greece	r	r	r	r	r	r	r
Hungary	r	r	r	r	r	r	**R**
Iceland	r	r	r	r	r	r	**R**
Ireland	r	r	r	r	r	**R**	r
Italy	r	r	r	r	r	r	r
Japan	r	r	r	r			**R**
Korea				**R**		**R**	**R**
Luxembourg	r	r	r	r	r		r
Mexico	r	r		r	r	r	
Netherlands	r	r	r	r	r	r	r
New Zealand	r			r	r	r	
Norway	r	r	r	r	r	r	r
Poland	r	r	r	r	r	r	r
Portugal	r	r	r	r	r	r	**R**
Spain	r	r	r	r	r	r	r
Sweden	r	r	r	r	r	r	r
Switzerland	r	r	**R**	r	r	r	**R**
Turkey	**R**	r	r	r	r	r	**R**
United Kingdom	r	r	r	r	r	**R**	**R**
United States					r		

Table 2. **Ratification of ILO fundamental conventions, situation as of June 2000**[d] (cont.)

(Bold print indicates ratifications since October 1995)

a) The table refers to the seven original fundamental conventions. The Worst Forms of Child Labour Convention (No. 182) was subsequently designated a fundamental convention by the ILO's Governing Body with effect from November 2000. As of mid-June 2000, the ILO had recorded ratifications of Convention 182 by 27 governments: Belize, Botswana, Brazil, Canada, Finland, Ghana, Hungary, Iceland, Indonesia, Ireland, Italy, Jordan, Malawi, Mauritius, Papua New Guinea, Portugal, Qatar, Rwanda, San Marino, Senegal, Seychelles, Slovakia, South Africa, Tunisia, the United Kingdom, the United States, and Yemen.

b) These ILO fundamental conventions were not included in the corresponding ratification table of the OECD's 1996 study.

c) Hong Kong, China is not an independent ILO Member state. However, it has notified the ILO of its intention to apply Conventions 29, 87, 98 and 105 (as of July 1997) and Convention 138 (as of April 1999).

d) Malaysia and Singapore have denounced Convention 105.

Source: ILO (1999b).

published statements (*e.g.*, observations or recommendations) of the ILO Committee of Experts on the Application of Conventions and Recommendations (CEACR) or the ILO Committee on Freedom of Association (CFA). In the absence of such statements concerning a given country, the table entries were updated based on published information confirmed in more than one alternative source such as the ICFTU's *Annual Survey of Violations of Trade Union Rights* and the US Department of State's *Country Reports on Human Rights Practices*. In a few cases, government submissions to the OECD provided information on recent changes. A conservative approach has been adopted in preparing the Annex Tables; generally, where the source criteria were not met, no change from the previous table entry was noted. In some cases the 1996 entry remained valid, but new or additional information of particular relevance was confirmed in 1999 and was included in the tables (shown in square brackets []). A very few corrections or additions to the actual 1996 entries were noted (shown in curved brackets {}).

Freedom of association

Annex Tables A.2 and A.3 give an overview of the main developments since the 1996 study concerning two important rights under ILO Convention 87: the freedom to form unions and the right to strike. Box 3 provides an assessment of the relationship between countries' level of economic development and their respect for freedom of association rights.

As can be seen from Annex Table A.2, the law and practice in the great majority of OECD countries remain generally consistent with the Convention's requirements concerning the freedom to form unions. Only about one-fourth of the other countries shown in the table conform with these requirements. Although for most countries there were no substantial changes noted during the years covered by this update, Korea and Indonesia in particular improved their performance. Those

Box 3.   **Freedom of association and the level of economic development**

Drawing on the information presented above and in the Annex Tables, Chart 1 highlights the relationship between the level of economic development (using 1995 GDP per capita as a proxy) and respect for freedom-of-association rights. The countries are categorised into four groups based on OECD Secretariat judgement concerning the extent to which they comply with the broad freedom-of-association requirements. The rankings from the 1996 study were generally maintained, except that Korea, Turkey and Indonesia were each advanced one group (to groups 3, 3 and 2, respectively) based on changes to their industrial relations system that have intervened since.

Group 1 includes countries where freedom of association is practically non-existent. Group 2 includes countries, where restrictions on freedom of association are significant (*e.g.*, due to stringent registration requirements, political interference or anti-union discrimination) or it is difficult to form independent workers' organisations or union confederations. In Group 3 countries, some restrictions exist but it is nevertheless possible to establish independent workers' organisations and union confederations. Group 4 consists of countries where freedom of association is generally guaranteed in law and practice; it includes all OECD countries (except Korea, Mexico and Turkey) as well as several non-member countries. The Chart highlights the positive association between the level of economic development and the respect for freedom of association. The update confirms the finding from the 1996 report that most economically developed countries enjoy above-average standards, while many of the poorest countries generally do not comply. However, there are outliers in Groups 1, 2 and 3, and there is also substantial dispersion in Group 4.*

---

*   The correlation coefficient is 0.61 between the country rankings (1 reflecting a low degree of observance of freedom of association and 4 reflecting a high degree) and levels of per capita GDP.

countries that fail to conform do so for a variety of reasons, and sometimes for multiple reasons. First, through interference or by limiting the ability of competing unions to function, some countries impose trade union monopolies or partial trade union "unity". In some cases (*e.g.*, in China, Egypt, Iran or Syria), union activity is limited to one officially recognised union or confederation often with some degree of political interference. In others, trade union unity is imposed on an enterprise, industry, occupational or geographical basis (*e.g.*, in Bolivia, Chinese Taipei, Malaysia or Zambia). Second, procedural or administrative requirements may make it difficult for unions or confederations to gain recognition (*e.g.*, Peru or the Philippines). Third, countries may excessively limit the right for public sector or "essential sector" (*e.g.*, utilities) employees to organise (*e.g.*, Thailand). Finally,

Chart 1. **Freedom of association and level of economic development**

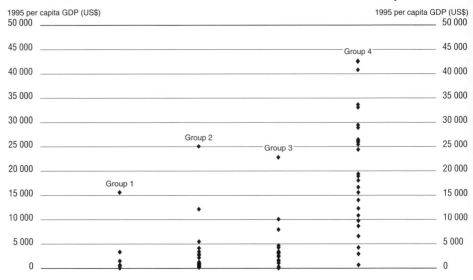

Note: The country groupings are composed as follows:
  Group 1: China, Egypt, Iran, Kuwait, Syria and Tanzania.
  Group 2: Bangladesh, Bolivia, Botswana, Chinese Taipei, Colombia, Guatemala, Haiti, Honduras, Indonesia, Jordan, Kenya, Malaysia, Mauritius, Morocco, Pakistan, Panama, Philippines, Singapore, Sri Lanka, Swaziland, Thailand, Uruguay, Zimbabwe.
  Group 3: Argentina, Brazil, Chile, Ecuador, Ethiopia, Fiji, Hong Kong, China, India, Jamaica, Korea, Mexico, Niger, Papua New Guinea, Peru, South Africa, Turkey, Venezuela and Zambia.
  Group 4: Australia, Austria, Bahamas, Barbados, Belgium, Canada, Czech Republic, Denmark, Finland, France, Germany, Greece, Hungary, Iceland, Ireland, Israel, Italy, Japan, Luxembourg, Malta, Netherlands, New Zealand, Norway, Poland, Portugal, Spain, Suriname, Sweden, Switzerland, United Kingdom, United States.
Sources: OECD Secretariat and UNCTAD (1999a).

several countries directly prohibit trade union formation in export-processing zones (EPZs) (*e.g.*, Bangladesh or Pakistan) or effectively do so by failing to ensure access or protection for union organisers (*e.g.*, Sri Lanka).

The situation is less clear with respect to the right to strike, in part because of certain exemptions that are permitted under the freedom of association as applied in ILO observations (*e.g.*, with respect to "public servants exercising authority in the name of the state"). Countries vary in their interpretation of these exemptions and, in some cases, there have been multi-year discussions between the CEACR and countries concerning the appropriate limits.[11] Annex Table A.3 presents information on changes in restrictions on the right to strike. As with the right to form unions, most OECD countries are in broad conformity with the convention (despite some reservations, particularly concerning public servants) Since the 1996 study, there have been some notable developments in OECD country practices. Korea has lifted some restrictions on third-party intervention and is gradually reducing the list of essential services where the right to strike is constrained by compulsory arbitration. The CEACR has expressed concern about restrictions introduced in Australia in 1996 that, "in the view of the Committee, excessively limit the subject matter of strikes".[12]

Only about one-fourth of the non-OECD countries are generally in conformity with the ILO requirements with respect to the right to strike; the majority impose significant constraints. Here again, there have been some changes in country practices. For example, a new Constitution in Ecuador recognises and guarantees the right to strike (except in essential services). Fiji partially reduced limitations imposed through strike procedures. South Africa has improved guarantees of the right to strike for most workers. On the other hand, the government in Niger has gained new powers to requisition state employees to work and Panama has imposed new restrictions on the right to strike in EPZs.

Annex Table A.4 highlights changes in the situation with respect to application of Convention 98, particularly in terms of promotion of collective bargaining and protection from anti-union discrimination. Here again, most OECD countries are broadly in conformity although there have been some issues raised by the CEACR. For example, the CEACR commented that certain provisions of the 1996 industrial relations legislation in Australia do not, in its view, "promote collective bargaining as required under Article 4 of the Convention".[13] In another case, the CEACR asked the Government of the United Kingdom to strengthen legal protections for workers against acts of anti-union discrimination by employers.[14] With respect to the non-member countries, the overall conformity with the convention appears to be better than in the case of Convention 87. About half of the non-OECD countries appear to be broadly in conformity, at least with respect to collective bargaining rights of recognised unions. However, there remain numerous restrictions (*e.g.*, in EPZs) and many countries fail to adequately protect workers against anti-union discrimination. Among the non-OECD countries, South Africa in particular stands out as having improved its practices since the 1996 report.

Forced labour, child labour and non-discrimination

The adoption of the ILO Declaration has heightened the visibility of these issues and the associated ILO conventions. As noted above and as can be seen in Table 2, there has been substantial progress since the 1996 study, with respect to the ratifications of the fundamental conventions related to these issues. However, there remain many difficulties in the *application* of conventions in all three of these areas. The ILO supervisory mechanisms have identified many continuing cases of non-conformity and abuses. Some progress has been made by focusing attention and technical co-operation on some of the worse cases. These issues are discussed in more detail in Part III.

Conclusions

Since the 1996 study was completed, the international community has made progress in developing an international political consensus with respect to the definition and recognition of core labour standards. The broad support for the ILO Declaration marked an especially important milestone in this regard whereby agreement was reached on language describing the fundamental principles and rights at work. With its emphasis on promotion and follow-up concerning these core labour standards, the ILO Declaration has helped to focus attention and efforts for improvement. It has strengthened ILO systems, in part by utilising existing constitutional provisions to extend the monitoring of the application of the fundamental principles and rights through a new reporting mechanism covering ILO member countries that have not yet ratified individual ILO fundamental conventions. At the same time, the ILO's efforts to promote ratification of the fundamental conventions – as an expression of the fundamental principles and rights – have also yielded positive results. The significant growth in ratifications implies broad recognition on the part of many countries that there is a need to conform to the standards as laid out in these conventions. However, there remains much work to be done in further extending the list of ratifications for each core convention if they are to be made universal. And, there remain substantial gaps between the ratification of conventions and the application and enforcement of their principles in practice. Indeed, it seems reasonable to conclude that improvements in practices have lagged the advances in the recognition of core labour standards.

Possible Links Between Core Labour Standards, Trade, Foreign Direct Investment, Economic Development and Employment

Introduction

This part of the update broadly follows the structure of Part II of the 1996 OECD study. The review of literature (concentrating on material since the 1996 study was completed) draws in part on the work of a consultant which is intended to be published separately as a working paper.[15] Some of the literature referred to in this part is not about core labour standards *per se* but about labour standards more generally. It was felt useful to address this literature in order to highlight the important distinction, for analytical purposes, between core labour standards and labour standards more broadly defined – a distinction that is often overlooked in the popular debate.

Part II starts with a discussion of the economic properties of core labour standards. It then addresses the relationship between the observance of core labour standards and trade performance. This section is then mirrored by a discussion of the relationship between the observance of core labour standards and patterns of foreign direct investment – including in export-processing zones. Attention then turns to the impact of trade on sectoral employment patterns and/or relative wages in advanced economies.

Part II concludes with a discussion of the pressures for, and economic effects of, international labour standards policy.

Economic properties of core labour standards

Since the 1996 study was completed, a number of papers have addressed the question of the relationship between core labour standards and economic efficiency and growth.

Stiglitz (2000), in challenging the neo-classical assumption that labour is just another factor of production, argues that the "high road" to economic development (which he takes to include the right to collective bargaining) can increase economic efficiency by, *inter alia*, promoting the increased buy-in by workers to the goals of the immediate work group. This, in turn, can lead to higher productivity via a "voice" mechanism. He also argues that collective bargaining can enhance the overall efficiency of the economy by facilitating income redistribution that would not occur, or would be more costly to implement, through the tax/welfare system. Stiglitz also cautions, however, that this is a delicate balance and that excessively strong unions can, through collective action, "hold up" the rest of the economy.

ILO (1998-9d) also addresses the economic benefits which can result from the enforcement of core labour standards. It concludes that:

- Child labour is detrimental to development since it means that the next generation of workers will be unskilled and less well-educated.[16]
- Collective bargaining and tripartite dialogue are necessary elements for creating an environment that encourages innovation and higher productivity, attracts foreign direct investment and enables the society and economy to adjust to external shocks such as financial crises and natural disasters.
- The discrimination faced by women and minority groups are important obstacles to economic efficiency and social development.

Drawing on the specific case studies, the ILO report also cites evidence of the constructive roles that the social partners have played in promoting economic development. It suggests that:

- In the Republic of Korea, tripartite dialogue at the national level facilitated the adoption of an all-embracing set of economic and social measures to cope with the 1997-98 financial crisis.
- In South Africa, social dialogue has played a crucial role in ensuring a relatively smooth political and economic transition in the post-apartheid era.
- The well-established tradition of social dialogue between the social partners in Switzerland lies at the heart of the country's economic success. The report finds that social peace is an important consideration when firms make decisions about their location, particularly in the case of high value-added activities that require large research and development investments and hence a stable long-term planning horizon.

Palley (1999) refers to evidence in the OECD 1996 study that, on average, countries which improved rights of freedom of association experienced an increase in GDP growth and manufacturing output in the five-year period afterwards [OECD (1996b), pp. 87, 131].[17] He draws attention to the limitation of this analysis in not controlling for other factors affecting growth. Palley seeks to address this limitation by controlling for the effects of earlier growth in the countries concerned and for the impact of growth elsewhere. For the countries examined, he concludes that improved freedom of association increased growth by between 1.2 and 1.4 percentage points on average.

32

Adherence to core labour standards can also affect a country's ability to withstand external shocks. A recent study [Rodrik (1997a)] considers the impact of adverse shocks that affected developing countries during the 1970s. The results of that analysis suggest that countries that develop democratic institutions – which here are taken to include core labour rights – before the transition to trade liberalisation will weather the transition with smaller adverse consequences than countries without such institutions.

Labour standards and trade performance

A principal finding of the OECD 1996 study was that there is no evidence that countries with low core labour standards enjoy a better global export performance than high-standards countries. This finding has not been challenged by literature appearing since the 1996 study was completed.

Two papers which have appeared since suggest that there could be a negative relationship between observance of labour standards and trade performance. Van Beers (1998) suggests that strict labour standards are associated with reduced exports of labour and capital-intensive goods produced with skilled labour. Jessup (1999) finds that, from 1989-1998, developing-country democracies' share of US manufacturing imports fell from 56.7% to 35.1%, while countries ranked as "not free" gained 10.6 percentage points and those ranked as "partly free" gained 10.9 percentage points. However, neither study addresses *core* standards. Van Beers uses a synthetic index of labour standards which includes working time, employment contracts and minimum wages while Jessup addresses the relationship between "democracy" and trade. For the purpose of analysing effects on trade performance, the distinction between core labour standards and other labour standards is crucial. Standards such as working time and minimum wages can affect patterns of comparative advantage, *e.g.* higher minimum wages are likely to affect trade performance negatively. But core labour standards, unlike minimum wages, will not necessarily affect comparative advantage negatively and indeed may have a positive effect.

Another study, Mah (1997), focussing on 45 developing countries, finds that each country's export share of GDP is negatively correlated with freedom-of-association rights and rights to non-discrimination. Exports are also negatively correlated with the right to organise and collective bargaining but the relationship is much weaker. However, as the estimated equations in this study do not have any control variables, it is not possible to quantify which characteristics are determining trade-related country differences. For purposes of this analysis we focus on workers rights, but it could equally be the case that other country characteristics are central to determining the volume of trade. Entering labour standards as an explanatory variable without properly controlling for other key variables is likely to yield biased estimates.

33

One approach which does not suffer from this deficiency is found in Rodrik (1996). In looking at a range of determinants of comparative advantage, Rodrik finds that labour standard variables are not statistically significant (though when the sample is divided into high- and low-income countries, the child labour variable becomes statistically significant in some specifications).

Another methodological weakness of studies on the links between labour standards and trade performance – highlighted in some recent work – arises from the fact that labour standards are generally set *endogenously*, as part of a broader industrial or development policy whereas the studies treat them as *exogenous*. Therefore, econometric results showing a positive correlation between export performance and suppression of labour rights may, in fact, be capturing the relative success of various development strategies rather than the impact of labour standards themselves.[18]

Labour standards and foreign direct investment

Empirical evidence

On the basis of observed patterns of international direct investment, multi-national enterprises invest principally in the largest, richest and most dynamic markets. With the significant exception of China, countries where core labour standards are not respected continue to receive a very small share of global flows. Rodrik (1996) suggests that countries with poor child labour practices attract less US capital than democracies that protect child workers. However, Jessup (1999) reaches a different conclusion. The difference is in part due to the fact that the two studies cover different periods, with Rodrik focussed on the 1980s and Jessup on the 1990s. However, it is also the case that Rodrik attempts to control for several factors that might be determining FDI along with democratic institutions. Jessup, by contrast, only presents raw data, without any attempt to control for other explanatory factors.

In sum, there is no robust evidence that low-standard countries provide a haven for foreign firms. This observation is illustrated in Chart 2 which shows the relationship between FDI inflows (averaged over 1995-98) and freedom-of-association ratings. The four groupings of countries are the same as those used in Chart 1 earlier). The chart shows a positive correlation between FDI inflows and respect for freedom-of-association rights. It is noteworthy that, because of the population size of China, the correlation coefficient is much stronger (0.41 compared with 0.20) if FDI inflows are calculated on a per capita basis. The small amount of FDI going to low-standard countries (except China) is relevant also to the role of export processing zones, with growing evidence that zones with poor working conditions are unlikely to attract *sustained*, long-term investment (see Box 4).

Chart 2. **Freedom of association and FDI inflows (millions of dollars)**

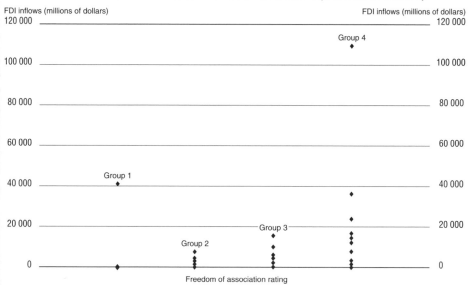

Note: The correlation coefficient between the country rankings and levels of FDI inflows is 0.2, *i.e.* showing a small positive correlation between FDI inflows and respect for freedom-of-association rights.
Sources: FDI data drawn from UNCTAD (1999*b*). For the composition of the Groups see Box 3 and Chart 1.

In terms of trends in international direct investment, investments in non-OECD countries have grown rapidly in the 1990s, from $28 billion in 1990 to over $150 billion at its peak in 1997. But these flows account for only a small share of total global inflows (23% in 1998 or roughly the same share as in the early 1990s). Furthermore, much of this investment outside of the OECD area is concentrated in only a few relatively large or wealthy countries, notably in East Asia and Latin America. Indeed, in 1998, the FDI gap among developing countries widened further, with the top five countries (China, Brazil, Mexico, Singapore and Indonesia) receiving 55% of all developing-country inflows and the 48 least-developed countries receiving less than 1%.

In terms of regional patterns, FDI flows into Latin America and the Caribbean in 1998 were 5% above those in 1997. Privatisation of service or natural-resource state enterprises is an important driving force of FDI flows into this region. In the wake of the financial crisis, FDI flows into Asia and the Pacific fell 11% in 1998, although FDI was the most resilient form of private capital flow. Contributing to this resilience were the availability of cheap assets, due in part to currency deval-uations, FDI liberalisation, and solid long-term prospects for the region. Africa

Box 4. **Export-processing zones**

Today, it is estimated that outside China there are about 850 EPZs worldwide, with 27 million people working in them. This compares with some 500 zones at the time the 1996 study was written. In addition, several hundred EPZs operate in China at the national, provincial and city levels. Most zone-operating countries are labour-surplus economies. China is the most significant labour-using country with 18 million people employed in firms with foreign investment, and many millions more in the Chinese firms operating in the zones. It is followed by Mexico with some 900 000 created jobs. Other EPZs which have achieved significant job creation include Costa Rica (49 000), El Salvador (50 000), Guatemala (165 000), Honduras (60 000) Malaysia (190 000), Mauritius (80 000), Philippines (180 000) and Sri Lanka (268 000). Women account for a large share of the workforce in EPZs, *e.g.* they represent more than 80% in Central America and the Caribbean, 70% in Bangladesh (ILO, 1998c).

In most EPZ-operating countries, the national labour and industrial relations legislation is applicable to the zones. However, according to the ILO, labour ministries are generally not equipped to monitor the zones effectively, and often consider the zones as a low priority. In addition, many zones have their own systems of labour administration often staffed by ex-officials of the Labour Ministry. Moreover, a few countries exclude EPZs from the national labour legislation and system of labour-management relations. For example, Bangladesh continues to exclude EPZs from the scope of the country's *Industrial Relations Ordinance*. Pakistan has also excluded its zones from the scope of the *Industrial Relations Ordinance* and prohibited all forms of industrial action in them. Panama is the only country in Central America to have adopted special labour legislation for its EPZs, replacing the labour code [ILO (1998c)]. The ILO concludes that problematic factors such as high labour turnover, absenteeism, stress and fatigue, low rates of productivity, excessive wastage of materials and labour unrest are still too common in zones, [ILO (1998 b)].

There is some clear evidence of a positive effect of EPZs on employment. In addition, ILO (1998c) points out that wages in EPZs tend to be higher than average wages in the rest of the economy, a finding supported by Romero (1995) and Maskus (1997).

Moreover, the advantages of EPZs as a means of generating employment for low-cost, low-skilled labour are increasingly undermined by intensifying international competitive pressures. Host countries are recognising that fiscal incentives, effective infrastructures, and low-cost labour are generally not the decisive factors inducing long-term investments. "Smart" EPZs have adopted a number of strategies to ensure that labour productivity is continuously upgraded. Measures include incentives to investors to undertake human resource development. Examples include the Penang Skills Development Centre in Malaysia and the Skills Development Fund in Singapore, which provide financial assistance for training programmes (UNCTAD, 1999b).

ICFTU (1996) argues that zones with poor working conditions and low labour standards are likely only to attract firms that use unskilled labour and which will tend to move on to cheaper locations at their convenience. Maskus (1997) also notes that there is no systematic evidence that poor labour laws are effective in attracting investment; moreover, he states that over two-thirds of firms in EPZs are locally-owned or joint ventures between local and foreign capital.

(excluding South Africa) saw a modest increase in FDI inflows in 1998, but growth during the 1990s was much less than for FDI flows to other developing-country regions.

In sectoral terms, the largest share of global flows involves the service sector. For the most important outward-investing countries, services account for between one-half and two-thirds of total investment. For the OECD as a whole, investments in service sectors are roughly twice as important as those in manufacturing. Even within manufacturing, those sectors commonly associated with delocalisation – such as textiles and clothing – represent only a small fraction of the total. For US investors, for example, the textile and apparel sectors account for only one per cent of total manufacturing investment overseas.

Trade, employment and wages

Since the 1996 study was completed, a large literature has explored the linkages between trade, employment and wages. Indeed, the Secretariat has undertaken a major review of this literature and done some empirical work [see OECD (1997)]. There continues to be disagreement among researchers on the size of the trade impact on sectoral employment patterns and/or relative wages relative to the impact of other forces, *e.g.* technological progress, international migration and institutional changes.

Nevertheless, some research supports the view that technological change rather than trade is the main driving force behind increased demand for skilled workers in advanced economies:

- Berman *et al.* (1996) find that pervasive skill-biased technological change has led to a shift in labour demand towards skilled workers in twelve advanced economies, including Germany and the United Kingdom.

- Goux and Maurin (1997) find that in France the decline in demand for unskilled labour results primarily from changes in domestic demand that favour skill-intensive products.

- Robbins (1996) and Feliciano (1995) present evidence that income inequality has risen in some developing countries, including Chile, Columbia, Costa Rica, Mexico and Uruguay. If Stolper-Samuelson-type mechanisms (leading to factor price equalisation) were at work, the opposite trend should have occurred.[19] Developing countries that export labour-intensive/low-skill-intensive goods should experience a *convergence* in the relative wages of skilled and unskilled workers rather than growing inequality. The fact that relative wages in some developing countries followed trends in industrialised countries could reflect the presence of skill-biased technological change. Alternatively, it could indicate that, even if workers have benefited from trade liberalisation, such benefits have applied relatively less to intensive unskilled-labour sectors (like agriculture) than to skilled-labour sectors; or indeed that some of the assumptions of the Stolper-Samuelson theorem do not comply with reality.

Other studies confirm a role for trade in accounting for trends in earnings inequality, but the contribution is still limited:

- Borjas *et al.* (1997) find that high-school graduate wages in the United States relative to high-school drop-out wages rose by 11.5% between 1980 and 1995; immigration and trade are found to account for 40-50% of the change.

- Krugman (1995) argues that trade may have accounted for 15% of the growing wage disparity between high-school and college graduates in the US between 1980 and 1988.

- OECD (1997) presented econometric evidence that the fall in relative prices of import-competing sectors during the 1980s had a negative impact on the labour market situation of unskilled workers relative to skilled workers. The study suggested that the price changes may have accounted for up to ten per cent of the widening earnings inequalities in the United Kingdom and the United States and for cuts ranging from one to seven per cent in the relative employment of unskilled workers in nine Member countries.[20]

- OECD (1998a), drawing on various economic modelling work, concludes that 80 to 90% of the changes in wage and income distributions observed of late in OECD countries are attributable to factors other than trade with developing countries.

- Neven and Wyplosz (1996) find, that for Germany, wages and employment appear to be adversely affected by import competition. However, for Italy and the UK imports from advanced economies play a more important role in determining labour market outcomes.

Cline (1997) concludes, based on a review of the literature, that the preponderance of evidence indicates that international trade accounts for an increase in the return to some college education in the United States of about 2.5 percentage points over the decade of the 1980s. (Cline estimates that, in turn, the relative wage of workers with some college education to those with no college education rose 15% in the 1980s.)

Most of the research on trade, employment and wages reviewed above has focused on the potential role of trade in reducing the demand for unskilled workers in industrialised countries. However, Rodrik (1997b) draws attention to the impact of trade in increasing the *elasticity* of demand for labour and the resulting consequences for real wages. Trade provides consumers with the opportunity to substitute toward imports and away from domestic goods in the event that some factor price increase raises goods prices. An increased labour demand elasticity will, in turn, lead to greater volatility in wages and hours worked. It would also alter the bargaining environment between labour and management. Unfortunately, there is little evidence in the empirical literature yet on the magnitudes of these latter effects.

The economic effects of policies to promote international core labour standards

One source of the pressures in some developed countries for international co-ordination or harmonisation of core labour standards is the fear of a "race to the bottom". However, a number of recent studies [Wilson (1996), Lawrence (1996), Srinivasan (1996) and Krueger (1996)] point to constraints on such a race in fairly competitive markets:

- Any firm that attempts to gain a competitive advantage by cutting benefits without paying increased money wages is essentially trying to cut wages below the workers' marginal value product. Competitive pressure from other employers will ultimately force the firm to return the total compensation package to the original level if it wants to be able to hire workers.

The outcome may, of course, be different where such competitive pressure is absent. Stiglitz (2000) notes that in the real world, there are costs to search, to finding out what wages other firms are offering, and even greater costs associated with moving from one employer to another. And, again, it should be pointed out that insofar as discussion of a "race to the bottom" focuses on wage levels, this is not directly relevant to the question of *core* labour standards (see earlier discussion under Trade Performance).

The empirical literature on this hypothesis is inconclusive. For example, Levinsohn (1996) finds very little evidence of labour standards affecting firm location. In contrast, Elmslie and Milberg (1996) claim to find considerable *historical* evidence of a race to the bottom. They observe that up until the US Congress passed the Fair Labor Standards Act of 1938, there was considerable competition between state legislatures in setting child labour laws. Oman (2000) concludes that there is little evidence in support of the stronger versions of the "race to the bottom" hypotheses, while pointing out that the evidence cannot tell us to what extent competition to attract FDI may inhibit a socially optimal *raising* of standards.

The corollary of the argument about constraints on a "race to the bottom" in a perfectly competitive market is that imposing labour standards on the operations of foreign firms will not alter relative competitiveness either. Even if labour standards are applied internationally, foreign firms can still only afford to pay workers their marginal value product. Underlying this proposition, however, is an assumption that productivity is unaffected by the imposition/enforcement of standards. As discussed above, there is literature (some of which was reviewed in the 1996 study) which argues that some core labour standards could have a favourable effect on productivity and therefore, potentially, on competitiveness.

39

Since the 1996 study was completed, there have been a number of papers on the economic effects of international labour standards policy:

Child labour

- Maskus (1997) suggests that a ban on child labour – where employers are forbidden from hiring children below a certain age – is more likely to be beneficial than a tax. Children forced from work will face the same options (in terms of alternative activities) as with a tax. But firms no longer have to pay a tax on children still working – a tax which must lower the after-tax wage of the working child.

- Basu and Van (1998) focus on the question of when an outright ban on child labour could be an effective policy tool. They argue that the labour market may be characterised by multiple equilibria – one in which wages are low and children work and another in which wages are high and children do not work. The effect of government intervention may then be to jolt the economy out of one equilibrium to another pre-existing equilibrium. They conclude that, if there are multiple equilibria in the labour market, a ban is a benign policy intervention. Basu and Van also conclude, however, that this situation occurs only in countries where labour productivity is moderately high and that if the market has only one equilibrium – which is likely in very poor countries – a ban can worsen the condition of poor households.[21] Basu and Van also address the question of implementation, pointing out that a ban on the import of goods which use child labour as an input could conceivably drive child labour out of export industries but would do little to prevent child labour in industries producing for the domestic market.

- Swinnerton and Rogers (1999) find that under the same conditions that Basu and Van identify for a ban to be effective, an equalising redistribution of income can eliminate child labour. Rogers and Swinnerton (2000) find that while in higher-productivity countries with child labour, a more equal income distribution can reduce or eliminate child labour, in low-productivity countries, a more equal distribution of income can exacerbate child labour. In the latter case, an equalising redistribution could lower the income of the highest-income families so that their children must work, without raising any other family's income by enough to enable them to take their children out of work. (The dividing line between "high" and "low" productivity economies is estimated at real GDP per worker of $10 000 – a conservatively high estimate.) Rogers and Swinnerton suggest that a policy implication one might draw from this analysis is that in low-productivity countries emphasis should be on productivity growth rather than on equity. Though, as they acknowledge, equity-inducing policies may, in certain circumstances, have the effect of raising productivity.

- Freeman (1996) has proposed the use of product labelling to deter the employment of child labour. Critics of the labelling approach have pointed out, however, that only about 5% of child labour is employed in the production of goods for export. Therefore, product labelling is severely limited in its potential to reduce child labour. Brown (1999) has shown that even a credible labelling programme introduces inefficiencies in the market and may have no effect on the total employment of children or the wages of their parents. Children can only gain if consumers are willing to pay a labelling premium that is large enough both to cover the additional cost of investing in adult-only technology and also bids up the cost of adult labour relative to child labour to the point where parents begin to withdraw their children from the labour force.[22]

- Brown *et al.* (1999) conclude that the only way in which a ban on child labour might work is if it is applied world-wide. In this case, the *world* supply of child labour will decline, thereby raising wages and rendering a high wage – with no child labour an equilibrium outcome. But in order for this strategy to work, the supply of child labour must be large enough relative to the market to alter the international wage structure; with the value of child labour estimated at some $300 billion, this seems unlikely [UNICEF (1994)].

- While much recent analysis suggests that trade sanctions will not improve the lot of children, Krueger (1996) argues that governments of countries in which children are employed may choose to change their laws rather than bear the costs of trade sanctions. As long as trade sanctions are only applied in cases where the cost of the sanction exceeds the benefit of the offending labour practice, the targeted country may choose to reduce child labour rather than suffer the trade sanction. Thus, the threat of sanctions could have positive implications for child welfare. Nevertheless, when considering this possibility, it is necessary that the gain from the threat of sanctions be weighed against the possibility that child labour practices will not change despite the penalties imposed by the rest of the world.

- Analysis suggests that trade interventions are not an *optimal* instrument to abolish exploitative child labour and expand human capital formation. The literature on optimal interventions suggests that the first best policy in these cases is to tackle the market failure directly. Recent literature provides some examples of such policies. For example, in Mexico, results from a programme subsidising families to keep their children in school show a return to school of about 20% of adolescents aged 12 to 16 years who were not enrolled in the previous year [see Mexico (1998)]. Basu (1999) suggests that such policies help countries avoid the child labour trap. In the absence of education, human capital formation is low. As a result, adult wages are low, thereby requiring children to work to supplement the family income.

Discrimination in employment and wages

- Maskus (1997) concludes that discrimination in employment may or may not expand exports. So the impact of labour standards on competitiveness is ambiguous. Moreover, from the point of view of the country where discrimination is occurring, discrimination is costly and inefficient. So it is in their best interest to eliminate discriminatory practices whether or not they are impelled to do so by international pressure. Nevertheless, there may be special interests that gain from continued discrimination that have political power to block reform. Foreign pressure may be useful in this case.

Freedom of association and the rights to collective bargaining

- Maskus (1997), Freeman (1993) and Corden and Vousden (1997) point out that the impact of trade sanctions when union activity is suppressed is hard to determine on *a priori* grounds. If unions offset monopsony power and bargain for a wage that is equal to the worker's marginal value product, the union's conduct may be welfare-enhancing. However, the impact of trade sanctions is ambiguous when union activity is suppressed. For example, suppose there is monopsony power in the export sector but unions are not permitted. In this case, a tariff that lowers the demand for the export good will also lower the demand for labour in the export sector. The monopsonistic distortion is thus intensified. The policy can only be considered a success if the threat of a foreign tariff leads the local government to relax the restrictions on union activity.
- Harrison and Leamer (1997) point out that unions function in the formal sector only. So sanctions may cause labour to be forced out of the export sector into the informal sector, lowering compliance even further. However, as noted by the World Bank (1995), the informal sector may have its own devices for mediating the mutual interests of workers and employers. Thus, issues of compliance may not be as relevant as in the formal sector.

Part III

Mechanisms to Promote Core Labour Standards Worldwide

This part sets out to review the current status of various mechanisms to promote core labour standards. The focus of the first four sub-sections is on: official mechanisms in place in the ILO, efforts to combat exploitative child labour, the engagement of international financial institutions and the WTO, and regional and unilateral trade-related initiatives. In the final sub-sections, mechanisms are described that address the conduct of firms, such as ILO and OECD instruments and private sector codes of conduct.

The ILO supervisory and promotional systems

ILO *enforcement of labour standards*

The ILO has at its disposal a variety of measures to monitor application of its Conventions. These include regular and special supervisory systems and *ad hoc* measures. These are complemented by provisions for follow-up including direct contacts and technical assistance (see Box 5).

- **The regular system of supervision** is based on the ratification of conventions by ILO member countries and their associated obligation to provide regular, periodic reports on measures taken to apply the various provisions.[23]

- **Special systems of supervision** include:

  1. *Article 24 procedures*, which provide for examination of representations by employers' or workers' organisations concerning a state's alleged failure to apply a convention that it has ratified.

  2. *Article 26 procedures*, which concern alleged failure to apply a convention effectively; they may be brought against a government by another government that has ratified the convention, by a delegate to the International Labour Conference, or by the Governing Body of the ILO.

43

Box 5. Direct contacts and technical co-operation

The ILO emphasises dialogue with Member countries concerning ratification and application of conventions. Where problems exist, the organisation has recourse to procedures for direct contacts and to technical assistance options. When the former is invoked, a representative of the ILO's Director-General is designated to confer with the key parties knowledgeable about a particular problem, including issues raised by the CEACR or cases before the CFA. This approach requires the consent of the country concerned and may involve visits to the country and consultations with senior government representatives. Recent direct contacts have involved Belarus, Bolivia, Colombia, Indonesia, Nigeria, Korea and Swaziland.

Through a new budget and restructuring effort beginning in 1999, the ILO has worked to renew its already substantial technical co-operation efforts. Much of the work for the period 2000-01 has been regrouped under eight "InFocus Programmes" covering priority issues. The goal is to improve the visibility and targeting of resources for these activities [ILO (1999d)]. Two of the programmes concentrate on core labour standards issues: the InFocus Programme on Promoting the ILO Declaration and the InFocus Programme on Child Labour (including the International Programme for the Elimination of Child Labour, IPEC, discussed below). The efforts under these programmes will be supplemented by continued provision of other types of technical co-operation linked to the full range of labour standards including the provision of legal advice on bringing national legislation into conformity and delivery of expert services through Multi-Disciplinary Teams serving 14 developing regions around the world.

---

3. *Freedom-of-association complaints*, which are handled through separate procedures and can emanate from organisations of workers and employers of the country concerned, from international organisations of workers and employers when one of their members is directly concerned, or from international organisations of employers and workers with consultative status at the ILO. These procedures may be invoked even where a country has not ratified Conventions 87 and 98.

- **Ad hoc measures are developed** as needed to deal with reporting on special labour standards issues (*e.g.*, apartheid was formerly covered) or to undertake direct contacts related to issues raised by the ILO supervisory bodies.

In terms of volume, the most comprehensive review of conventions is conducted under the regular system of supervision. As the number of ratifications and Member countries have grown, so has the workload for this system. Consequently, the ILO's Governing Body made the decision to adopt a staggered schedule of reporting requirements on the application of conventions. Generally, countries that have ratified a particular convention are requested to submit a report every two to five years; the reporting schedule has been adjusted several times over the years. Recently, with some 6 500 ratifications on record, the annual volume of submissions has amounted to some 1 500 reports.

The special supervisory mechanisms are invoked relatively infrequently. The ILO generally receives only a few Article 24 representations each year. The number of complaints under Article 26 is even smaller (in total, only 24 have been submitted). The Committee on Freedom of Association, on the other hand, receives numerous complaints. Since its creation in 1951, it has examined 2 060 cases concerning 137 countries.

Update on the operation of the ILO supervisory systems

In recent years, a number of initiatives have been undertaken to strengthen monitoring of core labour standards by the ILO (see Box 6). This section aims to provide an update on the functioning of the supervisory systems, with particular focus on results of the monitoring of core labour standards. It is beyond the scope of the present update to make a definitive assessment of the effectiveness of the ILO supervisory systems. However, in the course of 2000, the ILO is planning to undertake a review to assess the results of changes made earlier in the systems and to explore possible additional changes.

In terms of recent system outputs, it is useful to turn first to the CEACR, since it is concerned with the application of the full range of ILO conventions and recommendations within the framework of the regular supervisory procedure. During the period from 1995 to 1999 (inclusive), the CEACR *expressed satisfaction* in 169 cases where progress was made towards resolution of concerns identified through ILO monitoring. In an average year during this period, less than 10% of the CEACR individual country observations involved an expression of satisfaction with respect to a concern raised by the committee in earlier years.[24] While the majority of observations involved statements of new or continuing concerns, some of them were simply cautions, comments or requests for information that did not imply a negative finding. Since 1964, satisfaction has been noted in a total of 2 203 cases.

In 1999, the CEACR *highlighted progress* in 39 cases in 33 countries. Over half of these cases related to core labour standards: 17 concerned freedom-of-association, one concerned non-discrimination, three concerned equal remuneration, four concerned forced labour and one case concerned child labour (the minimum-age convention). At the same time, there was a substantial increase in the annual volume of CEACR observations between 1995 and 1999 with respect to the country practices concerning the fundamental conventions (160 and 265 in each year, respectively). This was partly a reflection of the increased numbers of ratifications for these conventions. The CFA has also remained busy, examining roughly 260 cases in 55 countries since 1995.[25]

Box 6. Strengthening the ILO mechanisms to monitor core labour standards

While the 1996 study noted concerns with respect to certain aspects of the coverage and reporting compliance under the ILO's regular supervisory system, there have been some improvements in recent years. First, although the system only applies to countries that have ratified the conventions, the number of ratifications has greatly increased (as noted in Part I). This increases the coverage of monitoring by the regular supervisory system. Second, the 1996 study noted that the system was "meaningful only if and when governments submit a report to the Committee of Experts". During the second half of the 1990s, the rate of submissions received by the reporting deadlines in advance of the CEACR sessions increased (from an average of 18% during the period 1991 to 1994 to an average of 28% during the period 1995 to 1998). Nevertheless, while many late reports eventually arrive in time for consideration at the scheduled CEACR session, others remain overdue or incomplete. This constrains the examination of issues by the CEACR. In the 1990s, for example, only about 60 to 70% of the reports each year were available in time for the scheduled CEACR session.[1] By this indicator, the timely availability of submissions at the CEACR sessions has deteriorated since the 1980s, when in any year 70 to 80% were received in time for the scheduled session. Thus, timely submission of reports remains an important area for improvement with respect to monitoring under the regular supervisory system.

The 1996 study cited measures proposed by the Director-General of the ILO to strengthen the supervisory systems.[2] These proposals were intended, in particular, to promote application of the principles of prohibition of forced labour and non-discrimination in employment in all member states, irrespective of their ratification of the corresponding conventions. A first idea was to extend the freedom-of-association procedure to these other fundamental conventions, but it was decided that this would not be workable.[3] As a result, a special reporting mechanism previously applicable only to Convention No. 111 was briefly instituted for non-ratifying countries. With the adoption of the ILO Declaration and its follow-up, this mechanism was replaced with an alternative, promotional approach based on an annual reporting procedure covering non-ratifying countries with respect to all four categories of fundamental principles and rights. This approach substantially broadens the monitoring of labour standards but, as with the regular supervisory system, it is dependent on timely and complete reporting by the countries concerned.

---

1. In cases where the reports are submitted too late for a particular session, they are considered in the following session.
2. These proposals were presented in ILO(1995) GB.264/6.
3. The principle of freedom of association is based in the ILO Constitution and applies to all Member countries. However, the forced labour and non-discrimination principles are embedded in conventions and not reflected in the same way in the ILO Constitution. Therefore, it was decided that they cannot be enforced through the constitution-based complaints mechanisms in cases where countries have not ratified the conventions in question.

Although the number of CEACR freedom of association cases has fluctuated from year to year, ILO experts note a trend towards improvement in that there is a substantial volume of cases resolved each year – progress acknowledged in the OECD's 1996 report as well.[26] In order to provide an estimate of progress against a standardised benchmark, the OECD conducted a review of non-compliance as reflected in CEACR observations during 1989 to 1999, taking into account the increases in ratifications and the changes in the volume and severity of cases. The review indicated that among countries covered in Table 2 that had ratified either Convention 87 or 98 there was only a slight improvement during the 1990s in the overall situation with respect to cases concerning Convention 87 and a possible worsening in the overall situation with respect to cases concerning Convention 98, as evaluated by the committee. (Details are presented in the Annex to this update).

With respect to the forced labour conventions, in 1999 there were 47 observations under Convention 29 and 44 observations under Convention 105.[27] While some recent observations apply to OECD countries, the most severe violations still concern countries such as Thailand, Bangladesh, Brazil, Haiti, India, Pakistan, Sudan and Peru.[28] Most severe cases relate to prison labour, compulsory labour, bonded labour (including children) or slavery. In addition to observations under the regular supervisory system, the special complaints procedures have been used recently in the cases of Brazil, Guatemala, Myanmar and Thailand.

Although the above-mentioned countries were also cited in the 1996 study, ILO experts note that several have shown some progress. In Brazil, the government has taken ILO comments seriously and has instituted new inspections and other measures to help locate, interdict and punish forced labour violations. Haiti appears to have made some progress in modifying previous forced labour practices in sugar-cane production. Pakistan now has an agreement with the ILO (under IPEC, described below) and UNICEF to halt use of child labour in the production of footballs and to provide schooling and income replacement. Sudan has established new mechanisms to track down and correct hostage-taking and slavery situations. Thailand has made progress by improving legislation and providing more enforcement, again, in part with technical assistance provided through the ILO (IPEC) as well as continuing supervisory comments. However, in Bangladesh, India and Peru, it appears that there is little perceptible progress.

In Myanmar, serious infractions against the forced labour conventions continued, despite a recent Article 26 procedure that mobilised substantial international pressure on the government to modify unacceptable practices. An ILO Commission of Inquiry (COI) in 1998 confirmed the existence of "widespread and systematic" forced labour practices in Myanmar and issued a set of recommendations intended to stop the abuses, particularly by the military. (Such commissions are reserved for grave and persistent violations of international labour standards.) In

June 2000, the delegates to the International Labour Conference voted by a wide margin to approve a resolution under Article 33 of the ILO Constitution, an article that had never before been invoked.[29] The resolution is intended to compel Myanmar to comply with Convention 29 (which Myanmar ratified in 1955). It specifies that in the event the government of Myanmar does not carry out the recommendations of the COI by 30 November 2000, a series of measures will be undertaken including: special scrutiny of the case in ILO bodies; a recommendation that the ILO tripartite constituents review their relations with Myanmar to ensure that they do not serve to perpetuate or extend the abuses; requests to UN bodies and other international organisations to reconsider their relations with Myanmar in case they may directly or indirectly abet the practice of forced or compulsory labour; and periodic reporting by the ILO Director-General to the ILO Governing Body on further developments.

With respect to non-discrimination in employment, in 1999 there were 20 observations concerning Convention 111, three of which concerned OECD countries. Under Convention No. 100 (on equal remuneration), there were 21 observations, 7 of which concerned OECD countries. With respect to the Minimum Age Convention (No. 138), there were 5 observations of which only one concerned an OECD country.

Follow-up to the ILO Declaration on Fundamental Principles and Rights at Work

As provided for in the Annex to the ILO Declaration, the follow-up is "of a strictly promotional nature" and clearly distinct from the ILO's supervisory systems. Its aim is to encourage the efforts of ILO members to promote the fundamental principles and rights at work, in part by identifying areas where ILO technical co-operation and advice "may prove useful to its Members to help them implement these fundamental principles and rights." The Declaration restates the ILO's obligation to assist its members in this regard.

The follow-up provides a mechanism for collection of information on needs, assessment of the effectiveness of ILO technical co-operation and determination of future priorities. Central to this process are two new annual reports mandated by the ILO Declaration but based on existing constitutional provisions. The first is a review of reports requested from member countries that have not yet ratified fundamental conventions; the second is a global report concerning application of fundamental principles and rights at work and technical co-operation priorities. The reporting mechanism is based on a cycle that, in the future, will begin each September with the submission of reports from non-ratifying countries. This is followed by an annual review of these reports by the ILO's Governing Body each March. The ILO's Director-General then submits a global report for discussion at the annual International Labour Conference each June. Based on this discussion, the Governing Body is to draw conclusions each November concerning the priorities and plans of action for technical co-operation for the following four years.

An important innovation under the ILO Declaration is the use of the provisions of the ILO Constitution [Article 19, 5(e)] to request the annual reports from non-ratifying countries on law and practice relating to matters covered in the fundamental conventions (discussed in Part I). The reports are based on four forms, each targeting key aspects of one specific category of fundamental principles and rights. The reports are compiled in the annual review by the ILO secretariat with an introduction prepared by a group of independent expert-advisors appointed by the ILO's Governing Body. The expert-advisors are to "[draw] attention to any aspects which might call for a more in-depth discussion".

The publication of the first annual review report in March 2000 constituted an early output of the first cycle of follow-up [ILO (2000a)]. The results of the first round of country reports were mixed. As noted by the expert-advisors, the ILO Declaration follow-up is "an evolving process" that will involve some fine-tuning. On the positive side, many countries provided useful and detailed information that will help them to set their own baselines against which to measure future progress. The expert-advisors welcomed the frankness of some governments in acknowledging areas for improvement and the creative approaches they sometimes adopted in overcoming difficulties in satisfying the obligations inherent in the fundamental principles and rights. There were other encouraging signs of growing commitment to the ILO Declaration. For example, fourteen countries that had abstained in the vote on the ILO Declaration submitted one or more reports[30] and two (i.e., Egypt and Indonesia) had ratified the seven fundamental conventions then in force.

Other results of the follow-up were less satisfactory. In particular, only about 55 per cent of the non-ratifying countries submitted reports despite the constitutional obligation to do so.[31] This is roughly 5 to 15 percentage points lower than the submission rate for comparable reports required of ratifying countries during the 1990s (see Box 6). Moreover, although the ILO Declaration is tripartite in nature, in many cases the social partners were either not involved or remained silent. Except in the case of freedom of association and the right to bargain collectively, there were relatively few comments submitted by employers' and workers' organisations. Also, a number of the country reports were evaluated by the expert-advisors as being "not particularly helpful" with respect to the purposes of the follow-up.

In their review of the reports, the expert-advisors noted several areas that countries identified for future action including implementing legislative reforms, protecting groups excluded under existing mechanisms (especially with respect to the informal sector), assisting persons with special needs such as the unemployed, addressing the situation of migrants and responding to the disruptive effects of armed conflict. The expert-advisors cited several themes in the reports with respect to technical co-operation needs including assessment of obstacles to ratification, assistance to strengthen social dialogue, development of promotional materials concerning the ILO Declaration, enhancement of statistical systems and labour inspectorates, reform of labour law, identification of measures to combat discrimination and further development of educational systems (especially for girls).

Although almost all governments affirmed their recognition of fundamental principles and rights, the reports also indicated many gaps or obstacles in implementation. For example, with respect to the freedom of association and the right to collective bargaining, some reports mentioned the exclusion of certain categories of workers (e.g., agricultural workers) or the imposition of single trade union structures. In the case of elimination of forced and compulsory labour, the expert-advisers lamented the weak content of the reports, but also noted the wide range of obstacles identified in the reports (ranging from the need for relatively minor revisions of legislation to problems embedded in particular political systems). With respect to the reports on the abolition of child labour, the expert-advisors complained about a lack of statistical data. The reports indicated a need to address the problem in a way that does not worsen poverty in the short term and that is sustainable in long term. The expert-advisors noted that legal prohibition of child labour is not enough to address the problem and were encouraged to see the range of complementary measures and social partnership discussed in the reports. Some countries noted the link between child labour and education, and cited the cost of providing universal education as part of the problem. The expert-advisors found the reports on elimination of discrimination to be limited in focus, highlighting legal measures (e.g., on prohibited aspects of discrimination), but failing to provide information on the actual situation with respect to discrimination. Indeed, the advisors were unable to draw conclusions on the real situation based on the information provided.

The expert-advisors recommended a number of concrete steps to improve the follow-up process, which were subsequently approved by the ILO Governing Body and are being carried out by the ILO Secretariat. For example, they suggested that the reporting forms might be improved by translating them into all official languages of the ILO and by requesting more detailed information on gender issues, social and economic conditions, freedom of association as it relates to the social partners, and measures aimed at the informal sector. Pending revision of the forms, they suggested that the ILO might provide a cover letter specifying the information that would be most useful. They encouraged greater engagement of the social partners in the reporting process. They also recommended that increased assistance be provided to governments in preparing the reports, particularly those that have not yet met the reporting requirements. One example cited by the expert-advisors was an ILO regional workshop on the Declaration held in Dakar in October 1999 which resulted in a relatively high reporting rate among participating countries. It was also the expert-advisors' suggestion to adjust the country reporting deadlines to fall in September so that the ILO would have more time to prepare the annual reviews.

The global report provides a dynamic picture of one of the four categories of fundamental principles and rights each year. This report is to serve as a basis for assessing the effectiveness of ILO technical assistance and determining technical co-operation priorities. It takes into account the annual review reports on non-ratifying countries as well as other official information such as that obtained through separate existing procedures (under Article 22 of the Constitution) covering the situation in countries that have ratified the fundamental conventions. The first report was released in May 2000 [ILO(2000*b*)] and focused on freedom of association and the effective recognition of the right to collective bargaining. Subsequent reports will address, in turn, the elimination of forced or compulsory labour, the effective abolition of child labour and the elimination of discrimination in respect of employment and occupation.

The first global report takes up the theme of globalisation and related changes in labour markets, and the implications for the application of freedom of association and the right to collective bargaining. The report highlights shortfalls in effective worker representation in certain areas including the informal sector. It then reviews the restrictions on the freedom of association and the right to collective bargaining, listing by name the countries where various types of shortfalls have been identified as well as countries where progress has been made. Using a case study approach the report reviews ILO technical co-operation and draws some general conclusions. The final chapter suggests some areas for technical co-operation (such as strengthening of institutions) for consideration by the Governing Body when it sets priorities under the ILO Declaration follow-up.

During the debate at the International Labour Conference, the global report drew a mixed reaction. Delegates praised the report for its identification of key issues and the advocacy it conveys. Several acknowledged that this was the first global report, prepared under tight deadlines and reflecting the first iteration of the process. At the same time, some delegates criticised the report for failing to present the most current factual information, questioned whether the report – being part of a promotional mechanism – should cite individual countries or sectors for falling short of the goals of the ILO Declaration, and found the analysis insufficient to enable the delegates to grasp cross-cutting trends that may not be evident from the anecdotal evidence and case studies. In his reply to the Conference, ILO Director-General Somavia acknowledged the comments received, but defended the naming of individual countries and sectors, saying "it is difficult to see how the [International Labour] Office can do credible reporting unless countries are identified and facts are stated." In the course of the debate on the global report, a number of speakers highlighted the benefits ILO technical co-operation brought to their countries or cited a need for additional support. The debate also made clear that the ILO Declaration has already awakened the interest of some donor countries.

ILO Working Party on the Social Dimension of Globalization

The ILO Working Party on the Social Dimension of Globalization (formerly the *Working Party on the Social Dimensions of the Liberalization of International Trade*) was set up in 1994. Over the last five years this Working Party has built a climate of confidence in its debate of the broad issues raised by globalisation. In particular a series of seven country studies was considered in 1999 by the Working Party, as well as an overview synthesis report.[32] The report, ILO (1998-9d) discussed earlier in Part II, emphasises that, although gains from globalisation can be discerned in terms of higher economic growth, the costs had probably been underestimated by the predictions made in the mid-1990s, notably in terms of increased income inequality and intensified labour-market instability. The March 2000 meeting of the Working Party was addressed by representatives of the WTO and Bretton Woods institutions who pledged their co-operation. At that time the ILO Governing Body decided to extend the life of the Working Party and to rename it to reflect the fact that the range of problems would extend beyond trade liberalisation. In this regard, the discussions in the Working Party will proceed along two lines: *a*) developing a method of analysis for an integrated framework of economic and social policies with a view to the promotion of decent work in the global economy; and *b*) fostering an understanding of the links between development and the fundamental labour standards enshrined in the ILO Declaration on Fundamental Principles and Rights at Work, starting with the question of freedom of association and collective bargaining.

Concluding remarks

The past three years have seen a strengthening of the ILO systems for monitoring the application of conventions. This has occurred, in particular, through the growth in ratifications and the further development of supervisory and promotional mechanisms. Moreover, the ILO Declaration on Fundamental Principles and Rights at Work has made an especially important contribution by extending the range of reporting to the application of the fundamental principles and rights. Although the follow-up mechanism has not yet worked through its first cycle, it has already generated a substantial volume of useful information. At the same time, it has become apparent that realisation of the full potential of the ILO Declaration will require fine-tuning of the follow-up procedures, increased engagement on the part of governments and the social partners and increased promotional activity.

The regular and special supervisory systems and the new mechanism under the ILO Declaration depend to a large extent on dialogue, moral suasion and technical assistance to bring results. A key element in the credibility of such systems for all of the social partners is the development of dispassionate, accessible and expert information on problems and solutions concerning labour standards. In this regard, the availability of extensive country-specific information from the CEACR and CFA is an important asset for the ILO, but it also poses a practical problem. While the direct access to this information has been greatly facilitated through various publications and through the user-friendly ILOLEX database that can be accessed via the Internet, it can be daunting for the uninitiated to navigate. Further development of the information system by the ILO will be required to ensure that key information gets to the users where it can do the most good in a timely fashion.

The approach of the ILO appears to work best in cases where the parties have a will to conform – within their economic possibilities – to the principles embodied in the ILO Conventions or where they are sensitive to public concerns when issues of non-conformity are raised. A future challenge will be to find a way for the system to focus international attention on the most serious infractions in a way that leads to early improvements, while maintaining efforts to promote increased respect for labour standards in the law and practice of Member countries in general.

The contribution of development co-operation programmes in eradicating exploitative forms of child labour

This sub-section updates the contribution of development co-operation programmes in eradicating exploitative forms of child labour.[33] After setting out the magnitude and societal effects of such forms of child labour, the interventions by bilateral donors to eliminate exploitative forms of child labour are elaborated on. Finally, the relevant programmes of international organisations are listed, e.g. the ILO's International Programme on the Elimination of Child Labour, the UNICEF Programme on Children in Especially Difficult Circumstances, and Country Assistance Strategies (CAS) and Child Labor Program of the World Bank and other international financial institutions.

Child labour is a complex issue that is closely linked to the stage of economic development. Krueger (1996) has demonstrated that there is a very strong negative correlation between child labour and per capita GDP. He suggests that when GDP reaches $5 000 per capita, child labour virtually disappears. Child labour can be viewed as the result of both politics and market failure. Poor families that send their children into the labour market may appear not to follow rational economic behaviour when education is clearly an investment with a high rate of return. In fact, the poor are making a rational choice, since income from child labour is often critical for family survival because of inadequate earnings of adult breadwinners. According to some studies, children contribute sometimes up to a quarter of household income. Nevertheless, exploitative child labour reinforces social and economic inequalities, and by denying access of the children in question to education it hinders their human capital investment which, in turn, reduces their expected lifetime earnings and has a negative spillover for society as a whole in terms of lowering economic growth potential.

The evidence is persuasive that in addition to enforcement of national legislation based on internationally recognised minimum standards, effective solutions to the problem of child labour should be based on poverty eradication, improving the situation of women, increasing access to, and the quality of education, and the provision of social security. These objectives should be central in any comprehensive development strategies aimed at promoting growth and poverty alleviation. Stable macroeconomic policies taking advantage of the opportunities offered by the global economy, alongside the promotion of an efficient public sector and a competitive private sector, should also be core components of effective strategies. Such strategies combined with strong political commitment can do much to reduce the extent of child labour and the harm it does to children. The design and implementation of specific programmes for the withdrawal of children from exploitation, and for preventing children from entering the labour force, require the active involvement of large sections of the population, including the children and their parents themselves.

The magnitude and nature of child labour

According to ILO estimates, 250 million children aged between 5 and 14 years are economically active in developing countries. Almost half of them are working on a full-time basis, while the others combine work with schooling or other non-economic activities. The extent of child labour varies regionally, with about 40% of children in Africa participating in economic activities, compared with 22% in Asia and 17% in Latin America. In absolute terms, Asia, being the world's most densely populated region, has about 54 million children working, compared with about 31 million in Africa. More boys than girls work – close to an average ratio of three boys to two girls. The relative level of the child workforce in specific economic activities varies considerably from one country to another.

Notable characteristics of exploitative child labour include the following: on average, almost three-quarters of children are working in activities related to the agricultural sector. However, the worst incidences of injuries and illnesses, in particular for girls, occur in construction, mining and the transport sectors [ILO (1999c); USDOL (1998)]. ILO survey results show that a large number of working children are affected by various hazards – more than two-thirds in some countries. Many (up to 20% in some instances) suffer injuries or illness.

Donor interventions

The donor community operates at the international and country level on the basis of partnership with recipients. Partnership approaches imply encouragement of recipient partners to formulate their own strategies – setting out the local priorities and instruments for implementing development. Such approaches involve consultations with civil society and external partners [OECD (1998*b*)]. In recognition of the fact that many factors contribute to child labour, partnership approaches and programmes tend to be comprehensive and often combine legislation and enforcement with practical support initiatives in a variety of fields. Since eliminating exploitative child labour is a vast and long-term undertaking, it is essential to set clear priorities and pay special attention to proper sequencing and co-ordination of preventive activities.

Donor programmes are often implemented in close co-operation with international organisations such as the ILO and UNICEF. The major thrusts of the partnership approaches to eradicate exploitative child labour are:

Reducing poverty

As stated above, widespread poverty is the major cause of child labour. Thus, poverty reduction is the most effective long-term approach. On a more specific level, donors try to aim their interventions at raising the earnings of the poor and in providing technical assistance to design targeted safety nets.

Educating children

Donor involvement also tends to be directed towards increasing participation of children in primary education with the objective of fostering human capital development. The DAC Strategy *Shaping the 21st Century: The Contribution of Development co-operation* [OECD (1996*a*)] commits donors to assist partners in achieving universal primary education in all countries by 2015.

Legislating and regulating child labour

Donor initiatives to strengthen enforcement of labour laws and regulations focus specifically on the most exploitative forms of child labour, such as children working in hazardous conditions, child prostitution and bonded labour. Stricter across-the board enforcement – as opposed to enforcement targeted at the most harmful practices – may actually damage those whom it intends to protect by reducing the income of poor families and forcing working children into more dangerous hidden forms of employment.

Providing support services

Direct support programmes tend to target children working in the urban informal sector. Some programmes also offer support to the families of working children. Programmes for both target groups involve providing supplementary feeding, night shelter, literacy programmes, and other venues for direct support.

Raising public awareness

Programmes to raise public awareness cover a wide range of activities aimed at improving the knowledge of work hazards and human capital loss associated with child labour. The heightened awareness enhances co-operation between local communities, NGOs, employers and governments to change harmful work practices and to address human capital loss.

International organisations

i) ILO

The ILO is responsible for carrying out the International Programme on the Elimination of Child Labour (IPEC) which was launched in 1992. The aim is to work towards the progressive elimination of child labour, giving priority to bonded child labourers, children in hazardous working conditions and occupations and children who are particularly vulnerable, *i.e.* very young working children. The programme represents an alliance of close to 90 countries, 19 of which are donors, and 4 contributing organisations. Total expenditure of the programme since its inception has amounted to more than US$57 million. The programme supports organisations in partner countries to develop and implement measures aimed at preventing child labour, withdrawing children from hazardous work through providing alternatives, and improving the working conditions.

IPEC applies a phased and multi-sectoral approach which consists of:
- creating an alliance against child labour;
- determining the nature and extent of the child labour problem;
- assisting in devising national policies to counter it;
- setting up mechanisms to provide in-country ownership and operation of national action programmes;
- promoting development and application of protective legislation;
- supporting direct action aimed at preventing child labour;
- and integrating child labour issues systematically into social and economic development policies and programmes.

An example of this type of approach is the Memorandum of Understanding (MoU) between the Bangladesh Garment Manufacturers and Export Association, UNICEF and the ILO, signed in 1995. The MoU includes a commitment to halt the hiring of under-age children, the removal of children under the age of 14 from garment factories and their placement in appropriate education programmes with a monthly stipend, as well as the offer to qualified adult family members to fill the vacated jobs. Social labelling schemes aim to promote companies' good public image by informing consumers of the conditions under which a product was made. These and other experiences are in UNICEF's view [UNICEF (1997)] encouraging signs showing that, when the problem of child labour is tackled on a broad front, considerable progress can be made to rid a sector of child labour in a given geographical area.

ii) UNICEF

UNICEF programming is guided by the UN Convention on the Rights of the Child and addresses the problems of child labour within the framework of its Programme on Children in Especially Difficult Circumstances (CEDC). UNICEF has developed a checklist of strategic options that could best meet the interest of the child. With respect to child labour and other forms of economic exploitation of children, it includes:

- expanding education opportunities either by "time off" to attend regular school or by providing schooling in the workplace;
- providing support services to parents, especially mothers;
- promoting stricter law enforcement against traffickers and those who "bond" child labour;
- providing services for children working on the streets;
- raising the age of marriage; and
- changing cultural values and social norms tolerant of economic exploitation of children.

UNICEF co-operates with other international organisations, governments and civil society in a wide variety of programmes to assist working children and their families. These programmes include formal and non-formal education and support services for working children as well as the creation of protected work alternatives. There are many examples of successful projects where rigorous inspections and enforcement of labour legislation have reduced child labour to minimal levels.

The role of international financial institutions in promoting core labour standards

) World Bank

Since the 1996 study was prepared, core labour standards and their operational implications have taken on heightened importance with the World Bank

57

within its mandate on poverty reduction and economic and social development. The World Bank has established a Labour Market Group within its Social Protection Network in 1998. The Group acts as a labour resource centre within the Bank by informing bank staff on labour issues, conducting staff training, co-ordinating co-operative initiatives with the ILO, and carrying out related activities. Furthermore, in the context of the International Development Association's twelfth replenishment, concluded in late 1998, a commitment was incorporated for the systematic consideration of core labour standards, with the co-operation of the ILO, in the preparation of the Country Assistance Strategy of borrowing countries.

Recognising that child labour is one of the most devastating consequences of persistent poverty, the Bank tries to help reduce exploitative child labour through its ongoing poverty reduction efforts in its member countries and through new initiatives aimed specifically at combating the most exploitative forms of child labour. These new initiatives include the establishment of a Child Labor Program in May 1998. The programme is based in the Human Development Network and is the focal point for Bank-wide activities, projects and policies.

The Bank's position on child labour includes:

- giving more focus to child labour issues in the policy dialogue with borrowing countries;

- improving partnership with other relevant international organisations and NGOs;

- raising the awareness and sensitivity of Bank staff of the issues involved;

- giving more emphasis to child labour issues in existing lending activities;

- requiring compliance with applicable child labour laws and regulations in specific projects where exploitative child labour is otherwise likely to occur and

- designing specific projects or components of projects to target the most exploitative forms of child labour, possibly starting with a pilot project in a country where child labour is seen as a serious problem [World Bank (1998)].

Examples of the Bank's efforts to reduce exploitative child labour include, for instance, projects in India that support primary school development by building national, state, and district managerial and professional capacity. The projects are targeted to disadvantaged children, including girls and scheduled caste and scheduled tribe students. Other projects aim to strengthen processes that promote economic development of women and create an environment for social change. One of the components supports income-earning opportunities for poor women, which will raise their incomes and thus expand the opportunities for their children to leave work and attend school.[34]

i)   *International Monetary Fund*

The International Monetary Fund (IMF) is increasingly paying attention to the social dimension of its lending programmes and economic policy advice. Recently, the IMF conducted an internal assessment of its performance in this area. The Fund now systematically tries to ensure that its policy advice, whether a condition for lending or not, does not adversely affect social programmes. The Fund also strives to strengthen social programmes in the context of macro-economic adjustment programmes. Furthermore, various approaches are being considered to enhance collaboration between the Fund and other international organisations, including the ILO, and between borrowing country governments and civil society, including labour unions.

ii)   *Inter-American Development Bank Group*

The Inter-American Investment Corporation, an autonomous affiliate of the Inter-American Development Bank Group (IDB) has adopted guidelines prohibiting the use of exploitative child labour and compulsory labour in projects it supports. The policy also requires borrower compliance with all domestic labour legislation, including those that enforce core labour standards. Furthermore, under IDB guidelines, project teams are responsible for conducting social assessments that include labour issues.

v)   *Asian Development Bank*

The Asian Development Bank (ADB) has taken the initiative towards designing a framework for operations on social protection and social safety nets. Work carried out since 1998 has enabled agreement to be reached on a definition of social protection as the set of policies and programmes designed to promote effective labour market policies; protect individuals from the risks inherent in labour market participation; and provide a basis of support to individual participants. This framework will be used in the Bank and member countries to design or redesign programmes for social protection.

)   *African Development Bank*

The African Development Bank (AfDB) conducted in 1998 an extensive review on how to incorporate core labour standards into its policies and programmes. In response to the report, bank management has agreed to pursue a three-part strategy consisting of *i)* sensitising Bank staff on core labour standards; *ii)* playing an active role in the debate on core labour standards; and *iii)* incorporating core labour standards into Bank planning documents, including Country Strategy Papers. The bank has already begun to implement the recommendation derived from this review by supporting core labour standards in its newly issued governance policy and its revised education and agriculture sector policies.

59

Concluding remarks

Since the 1996 study was prepared, the contribution of development co operation programmes in eradicating exploitative forms of child labour has become more focussed and results-oriented. The aid community has reflected on the lessons learned and put forward comprehensive strategies to tackle the prob lem. Effective development co-operation can and has made a real difference in achieving the goal of eradicating exploitative forms of child labour. But this goal cannot be achieved by aid alone. The most important contribution is being made by the people and the governments of the developing countries themselves. But where these efforts are being made, support from the industrialised countries and international organisations is needed and has been extended to make a differ ence in reducing poverty, educating children, legislating and regulating child labour, providing support services and raising public awareness.

Labour standards and the WTO

There have been a number of important developments under this heading since the 1996 study. In December 1996, Trade Ministers issued a Declaration on core labour standards at the First WTO Ministerial Meeting, held in Singapore [WTO (1996)]:

> "We renew our commitment to the observance of internationally recognized core labour standards. The International Labour Organization (ILO) is the competent body to set and deal with these standards, and we affirm our support for its work in promoting them. We believe that economic growth and development fostered by increased trade and further trade liberaliza tion contribute to the promotion of these standards. We reject the use of labour standards for protectionist purposes, and agree that the comparative advantage of countries, particularly low-wage developing countries, must in no way be put into question. In this regard, we note that the WTO and ILO Secretariats will continue their existing collaboration."

Repeated references have been made since then to this Ministerial statement of sup port for the ILO as the competent body to set and deal with core labour standards.

In preparing their inputs for the Third WTO Ministerial Declaration for Seattle in December 1999, the United States, the European Union and Canada submitted proposals to address trade and labour questions. The United States proposed the adoption of a forward work programme to address trade issues relating to labour questions including the establishment of a Working Group on Trade and Labour to operate under the supervision of the WTO General Council [WTO (1999a)]. The European Communities proposed that the Third WTO Ministerial adopt a decision to establish a joint ILO/WTO Standing Working Forum on trade, globalisation and labour issues [WTO (1999b)]. Its aim would be to promote a substantive dialogue between all interested parties, focussing on an examination of the relationship between trade liberalisation, development and core labour standards. It should explicitly exclude any issue related to trade sanctions. Canada proposed the establishment of a WTO working group to report to the next Ministerial Conference on the relationships between appropriate trade, developmental, social and environmental policy choices in the context of the experiences of and challenges faced by all WTO members in adjusting to globalisation [WTO (1999c)]. A purpose of the working group would be to help ensure that the WTO works in co-ordination with other international organisations, including the ILO.

These proposals were discussed in Seattle and attracted opposition from a number of WTO Members. Reactions in Seattle were particularly strong against suggestions for the use of trade sanctions against those who violate core labour standards. In view of the fact that no Ministerial Declaration was concluded, the future of the proposals to set up working groups appears uncertain. Another suggestion made by the future head of the WTO would involve a high-level dialogue convened by a "neutral" institution such as UNCTAD or ECOSOC reviewing the relationship between labour standards and the trading system, including the question of social safety nets.

Since the 1996 study, matters relevant to labour standards have been raised routinely by a few OECD Member countries in the course of the reviews in the WTO Trade Policy Review Body (TPRB). On the other hand, developing country participants in the TPRB have repeatedly expressed the view that issues relating to core labour standards should be raised in the ILO rather than the WTO. In October 1999 in its Report to the WTO Ministerial, the TPRB reconfirmed the objectives and coverage of the Trade Policy Review Mechanism, set out in Annex 3 of the Marrakesh Agreement.

Regional and unilateral government actions

The North American Agreement on Labor Cooperation (NAALC)

The 1996 study describes the procedures by which the NAALC, a side agreement to the North American Free Trade Agreement (NAFTA), promotes enforcement of existing labour laws in the three Member countries.

Between the time the 1996 study was completed and the end of 1999, a further 17 public communications had been received by the National Administrative Offices (NAOs) to the NAALC (as compared with five submissions made in 1994 and 1995). Of these 17, ten have been received by the US NAO – eight relating to issues arising in Mexico and two in Canada. Four communications were received by the Mexican NAO and related to labour law issues in the United States. Three public communications were received by the Canadian NAO; two related to issues arising in the US and one in Mexico.

61

Since 1996, most of the cases (see Table 3) involve allegations of infringement of the rights to freedom of association and right to organise or the right to bargain collectively, including the right to strike. Several involve prevention of occupational injuries and illnesses. Others concern illegal child labour; protection of migrant labour or issues of gender discrimination.

Canada-Chile Agreement on Labor Cooperation

The provisions of the Canada-Chile Agreement on Labor Cooperation, which entered into force in 1997, mirror those of the NAALC.

Mercosur

In December 1998, the Presidents of the Mercosur countries (Argentina, Brazil, Paraguay and Uruguay) signed the "Declaración Socio-laboral del Mercosur". A general objective of the Declaration is to accompany the southern cone regional integration process with a social framework. The Declaration's 25 articles are grouped in three sections dealing with individual rights (*e.g.* non-discrimination; elimination of forced labour; child labour); collective rights, both of employers and of workers (freedom of association; collective bargaining; strikes etc); and procedures addressing implementation and follow-up. Whilst the Declaration does not *per se* set regional norms, Mercosur States have committed to promote the Declaration's principles according to their national legislation and practice, as well as per collective conventions and agreements. A tripartite Social and Labour Commission is provided for. Amongst its six main attributions are those of taking up submissions concerning difficulties in implementing the Declaration and providing clarifications about the Declaration.

SADC

In 1996, the 14-member Southern African Development Community (SADC) established the Employment and Labour Sector (ELS). Operating on a tripartite basis, it reports to the SADC Council of Ministers. Based on an earlier initiative of the trade union movement concerned about regional integration, ELS set about to formulate the Social Charter of Fundamental Rights. Following tripartite consultations in each of the Member states a draft text was agreed by the ELS and is awaiting final approval by the Council of Ministers. The Social Charter commits SADC member states to observe a number of basic rights and principles, *e.g.* freedom of association and collective bargaining and equal treatment for men and women. It also commits member states to ratify and implement the seven ILO fundamental conventions. While implementation would be left to national tripartite institutions, members would be required to submit regular progress reports on the implementation of the Social Charter to the annual tripartite ELS meeting.

Table 3. **NAALC submissions and outcomes, 1996-1999**

Communication received	Submitted to	Submitter	Issue/Principle	Ministerial Consultations	Outcome/Follow-up Activities
9601	US NAO	International Labor Rights Fund, Human Rights Watch/ America, National Association of Democratic Lawyers	Freedom of Association/Right to Organise	Yes	Conference on International Treaties and Labor Law
9602	US NAO	Communications Workers of America (CWA)	Freedom of Association/Right to Organise	No	Withdrawn
9701	US NAO	International Labor Rights Fund, Human Rights Watch/ America, National Association of Democratic Lawyers	Employment discrimination	Yes (October 1998)	Action plan on pregnancy discrimination; Conference on Rights of Women. Outreach sessions on US and Mexican laws protecting women workers held or planned.
9702	US NAO	National Association of Democratic Lawyers, Support Committee for Maquiladora, International Labor Rights Fund, Union of Metal, Steel, Iron and Allied Workers (STIMAHCS)	Freedom of Association/Right to Organise Occupational Safety later added	Accepted by Mexico in Oct. 98	Pending
9703	US NAO	United Steelworkers of America, AFL-CIO/ CLC, United Electrical, Radio and Machine Workers of America (UE), International Brotherhood of Teamsters	Freedom of Association/Right to Organise; Right to Bargain Collectively; Prevention of Occupational Injuries and Illnesses	Requested in Aug. 98	Pending
98-1	Canadian NAO	United Steelworkers of America, (Canada Office), and 11 other unions and 31 concerned organisations (Similar to US NAO 9703)	Freedom of Association/Right to Organise; Prevention of Occupational Injuries and Illnesses	Requested; agreed to by Mexico	Pending

63

Table 3. **NAALC submissions and outcomes, 1996-1999** (*cont.*)

Communication received	Submitted to	Submitter	Issue/Principle	Ministerial Consultations	Outcome/Follow-up Activities
9801	Mexican NAO	Oil, Chemical and Atomic Workers International, Local 1-675, OCAW; *Sindicato de Trabajadores de Industría y Comercio "6 de octubre"; Unión de Defensa Laboral Comunitaria; Comité de Apoyo para Los Trabajadores de las Maquiladoras*	Freedom of Association/Right to Organise, Right to Bargain Collectively, Minimum Employment Standards and Prevention of Occupational Injuries and Illnesses	Agreed to by US	Pending
9802	Mexican NAO	*Frente Auténtico de Trabajo* (FAT); *Unión Nacional de Trabajadores* (UNT); *Frente democrático campesino* (FDC); STIMAHCS	Freedom of Association/Right to Organise, Right to Bargain Collectively, Minimum Employment Standards, Prevention of Occupational Illness and Injuries, Protection of Migrant Workers, Elimination of Employment Discrimination	Requested; agreed to by US in Sept. 99	Pending
9803	Mexican NAO	*Confederación de Trabajadores de México* (CTM)	Protection of Migrant Workers, Minimum Employment Standards, Elimination of Employment Discrimination, Prevention of Occupational Injuries and Illnesses, Compensation in Cases of Occupational Injuries and Illnesses	Requested by Mexico in Nov. 99	Pending

Table 3. **NAALC submissions and outcomes, 1996-1999** (*cont.*)

Communication received	Submitted to	Submitter	Issue/Principle	Ministerial Consultations	Outcome/Follow-up Activities
9801	US NAO	Association of Flight Attendants, AFL-CIO	Right to strike	No	US NAO rejected communication for review but agreed to conduct a research project on how 3 countries reconcile the right to strike and national interests of safety, security and general welfare.
9802	US NAO	Florida Tomato Exchange (non-profit agricultural co-operative association)	Illegal child labour practices (on vegetable farms in Mexico)	No	US NAO closed the file based on lack of sufficient information to proceed.
98-2	Canadian NAO	Yale Law School Workers' Rights Project; American Civil Liberties Union Foundation Immigrants' Rights Project; a number of other civil rights organisations and trade unions	US minimum employment standards. (Previous MOU between DOL and Immigration and Naturalization Service (INS) limited DOL inspectors to investigate wages and hours complaints)	No	File closed in view of new MOU between US DOL and INS
9804	Mexican NAO	(Identical to Canadian 98-2)	Idem to above	No	US NAO sent Mexican NAO the new MOU between DOL and INS modifying contested one.
9803	US NAO	International Brotherhood of Teamsters, Teamsters Canada, Quebec Federation of Labor, Teamsters Local 973 (Montreal) and International Labor Rights Fund	Plant closures with anti-union motivations and unwarranted delays in union certification procedures	No	It was agreed that a Quebec government council would commence a broad study of the provinces' labour legislation including the issue of sudden anti-union plant closures.

Table 3. **NAALC submissions and outcomes, 1996-1999** (*cont.*)

Communication received	Submitted to	Submitter	Issue/Principle	Ministerial Consultations	Outcome/Follow-up Activities
9804	US NAO	Organization of Rural Route Mail Carriers and other labor organisations in the US, Mexico and Canada	Right to unionise and bargain collectively	No	US NAO has not accepted communication for review on basis that the submission did not raise questions regarding the application or enforcement of the law and did not constitute a failure to comply with NAALC obligations.
99-1	Canadian NAO	The (US-based) Labor Policy Association and (a US-based manufacturer), the EFCO Corporation	Freedom of association and right to organise unions	None announced	Submitters told communication not accepted for review, as information did not indicate a failure to comply with the NAALC. Pending
9901	US NAO	Association of Flight Attendants, AFL-CIO and *Associación syndical de sobrecargos de aviación* (ASSA)	Rights of freedom of association and to organise unions	None announced	Pending

Source: NAALC information submitted to OECD Secretariat.

Agreements with the European Community

The partnership agreement between the African, Caribbean and Pacific States and the European Community and its Member States, whose negotiations were concluded in February 2000, included a reaffirmation of the signatories' commitment to core labour standards, as defined by the relevant ILO Conventions. The Agreement on Trade, Development and Cooperation between the European Community and its Member States and the Republic of South Africa concluded in July 1999 included a similar reaffirmation.

Labour standards and trade preferences

i)   US *legislative initiatives, including the* GSP *Program*

Legislation designed to promote internationally-recognised workers' rights in developing countries has been added to several US trade and aid programmes over the past 15 years (see Box 7). Among these programmes, the GSP is the most important in terms of promoting better labour standards. The US GSP scheme was first implemented on 1 January 1976 and re-authorised in 1984, amending the original GSP provisions by adding additional eligibility criteria for beneficiary countries, including new criteria regarding worker rights. The criteria in the 1984 GSP legislation stipulated that a country may not be designated a beneficiary developing country "if such country has not taken or is not taking steps to afford internationally-recognised worker rights to workers in the country (including any designated zone in the country)". The GSP workers' rights are based on the ILO conventions but do not replicate them. Since 1993, the GSP Programme has been extended several times. In November 1999, the Congress re-authorised the GSP Programme through 30 June 2001 and also applied it retroactively to its expiration date of 30 June 1999 at a total cost of $798 million.

From 1984 through 1999, 47 countries have been named in one or more petitions citing labour rights abuses according to the GSP Law. Since the 1996 report, seven more countries have been named (Belarus, Swaziland, Indonesia, Guatemala, Cambodia, Bangladesh and Thailand); four of them had been the subject of previous petitions, three were new (Belarus, Cambodia and Swaziland).

The influence of the GSP depends not only on the possible withdrawal of a country's tariff preferences, and the threat to do so, but also on the review process itself which may include consultations with the country in question as well as drawing public attention to a country's labour practices.

The primary objective of the GSP review is to encourage the promotion of improved workers' rights in beneficiary countries. According to the ICFTU, the threat of withdrawal of US GSP brought changes to the labour code and improved

67

Box 7. **Trade and labour rights in the United States: child labour and prison labour**

Child labour

Since the drafting of the 1996 study, there have been several developments in the United States concerning trade and child labour. Through the efforts of Senator Harkin and other sponsors, whose legislative initiatives were described in the 1996 study, a series of Congressionally-mandated annual reports entitled *By the Sweat and Toil of Children* has for the past five years been looking at the child labour situation around the world. The most recent of these – *Efforts to Eliminate Child Labor* – concentrates on the child labour population in 16 developing nations, the relevant laws and the state of primary education and child labour projects in place.

The 1930 US Tariff Act, Section 1307, forbids imports of goods produced with prison or indentured labour. But the law does not specify whether this covers forced or indentured child labour. In October 1997, as a rider to appropriations legislation for the US Customs Service (Department of Treasury), Congress legislated that Section 1307 provisions should also forbid importation of goods made using forced or indentured child labour. Subsequently, Congress renewed this legislation, although to date it has never amended the original Statute. In 1998, the Secretary of the Treasury sent a letter to Senator Harkin announcing that the Treasury would continue to interpret Section 1307 as prohibiting imports of goods made with forced or indentured child labour. The US Administration uses a consultative body, whose membership includes human rights organisations, labour unions and business interests, to advise the Treasury on how to enforce the US ban on imports of goods made with forced or indentured child labour. Additional money has been appropriated to assist Customs authorities in the enforcement of this provision.

In June 1999, President Clinton signed an Executive Order, "Prohibition of Acquisition of Products Produced by Forced or Indentured Child Labor", stating that US executive agencies are to enforce laws prohibiting the manufacture or importation of goods mined, produced or manufactured by forced or indentured child labour. Excluded from the scope of the Executive Order are contracts with parties to NAFTA or the WTO Agreement on Government Procurement.

Prison labour

As a follow-up to the 1992 MoU with China on prison labour exports, the US negotiated a Statement of co-operation (SOC) in 1995. This SOC was designed to tighten up the 1992 MoU by allowing US embassy officials in Beijing, upon request, to visit prisons suspected of operating factories producing goods for export. This has been a point of some contention when the US Congress has held hearings in the past on the renewal of China's MFN status. This authority also derives from Section 1307 of the 1930 US Statute mentioned above.

rights to collective bargaining and freedom of association for workers in a number of countries of Central America and the Caribbean, most notably in the Dominican Republic.

Prior to 1996, eleven countries had been fully removed or suspended from GSP pursuant to a worker rights review. Five of these countries (Chile, Central African Republic, Paraguay, Romania and Mauritania) have been reinstated to GSP after losing benefits, so there can be some leverage even after benefits are withdrawn. Nicaragua later received a waiver to make it eligible for CBI benefits. Pakistan has been partially suspended from GSP because of worker rights violations.[35]

ii)   The EC GSP

The direct link between trade and core labour standards, established in the 1994 GSP of the European Communities,[36] was reiterated in the 1998 scheme applying from 1 July 1999 to 31 December 2001.[37] The EC approach is based on special incentives which constitute an additional element to the basic GSP offer. These incentives are made available to those beneficiary countries which apply for them and can prove that they effectively implement certain core labour standards. On the other hand, the EC regulation provides for the possibility of disincentives, under certain circumstances, in the form of suspension of GSP benefits.

The incentives for labour rights may be granted only to countries which request them and provide proof that they implement legislation incorporating the substance of the standards laid down in ILO Conventions No. 87, 98 and 138. Requests for application of the social incentives must be subject to a publication procedure. The decision on whether to grant additional incentives must be taken within a year following the receipt of the request after the Commission has examined the request and verified the received information. In the case of a favourable decision, additional preference can be granted only to certain sectors. If the Commission decides not to grant the special incentive arrangement or to exclude some sectors, it has to explain the reason for its decision to the country concerned, on request. In a second stage, the Commission grants the additional margins further to a certification system (guaranteeing that the products and their components have been manufactured in the country).[38]

The republic of Moldova[39] and the Federation of Russia[40] have applied for additional benefits under the social clause. These requests are at present under examination by the Commission.

On the other hand, a temporary suspension in whole or in part of the preference scheme can be decided in circumstances such as the practice of slavery or forced labour or export of goods made by prison labour. The temporary withdrawal is not automatic but subject to a procedural requirement. Member states or any natural or legal persons or associations can notify such practices to the Commission, which then initiates consultations with the concerned parties before deciding whether to open an investigation. The suspension measure, if any, cannot be implemented before a year of investigation and a decision by a qualified majority of the Council. The Commission shall seek all necessary information and verify the information with economic operators and the competent authorities of the beneficiary countries.

On 24 March 1997, based on a complaint from the ETUC and the ICFTU, the Council temporarily withdrew access from Myanmar to the tariff preferences under both the industrial and the agricultural GSP-schemes because of its use of forced labour.[41]

The European Union has raised the idea that its GSP incentive clause could be a model for a multilateral system of additional preferences granted to developing countries which uphold core labour standards. It is suggested that the attractiveness of preferences could be improved in this context.

International standards for the conduct of firms

The ILO Tripartite Declaration of Principles concerning MNEs and Social Policy

The sixth review of the ILO Tripartite Declaration was concluded in 1997. The analysis concluded that "over the years there has been a fairly wide degree of observance of the Tripartite Declaration and that, on the whole, the social and economic effects of MNEs have been positive". The study pointed out that MNEs and joint ventures with foreign participation generally showed better performances in the areas of pay, working conditions, occupational safety and health, training and labour relations than local enterprises in a number of countries. While the overall conclusion of the study was positive, the analysis expressed concern over future employment security in response to the increase of mergers and acquisitions and privatisation. With respect to export processing zones, the report concluded that the experiences have been mixed.

The OECD Guidelines for Multinational Enterprises

The OECD Guidelines are non-binding recommendations addressed to MNEs by adhering governments (those of OECD countries and of four non-member countries: Brazil, Argentina, Chile and the Slovak Republic). The recommendations – which cover such areas as employment and industrial relations, environment, combating bribery, competition, disclosure and taxation – seek to ensure that MNEs operate in harmony with government policies, to strengthen the basis of mutual confidence between enterprises and the societies in which they operate and to help improve the foreign investment climate. The Guidelines were originally adopted by the governments of OECD Member countries in 1976 as part of the OECD Declaration on International Investment and Multinational Enterprise. The Declaration is a broad set of instruments defining commitments of governments and of international business. Its other instruments contain commitments by governments to provide national treatment for foreign-controlled enterprises, to avoid conflicting requirements and to co-operate regarding incentives and disincentives for foreign investment.

In June 2000, the CIME completed a comprehensive review of the Guidelines. The review covered the recommendations to enterprises, the follow-up procedures and the geographical applicability of the Guidelines.

While recognising the value of stability in the text and follow-up procedures, the Review involved a thorough reconsideration of the Guidelines so as to ensure their continued relevance and effectiveness in light of the changing needs of the global economy. Many long-standing features of the Guidelines were maintained in the revised recommendations and implementation procedures. Observance of the Guidelines by firms is still voluntary, but adhering governments are committed to furthering their observance. The revised implementation procedures maintain the Guidelines' focus on National Contact Points – government offices in adhering countries that are charged with promoting the Guidelines – but seek to improve the functioning of these offices. The revised Guidelines clarify the shared views of adhering governments on the role and responsibilities of the National Contact Points and of the CIME and enhance their transparency and accountability. The changes to the Guidelines recommendations reinforce the core elements – economic, social and environmental – of the sustainable development agenda. The revised recommendations make it clear that they apply to enterprises operating in or from adhering countries and that they are relevant for their operations in all countries.

One chapter of the Guidelines addresses employment and industrial relations. It urges firms to: respect workers' rights to freedom of association; to provide information and facilities to employee representatives; to communicate effectively with employees so as to enable them to obtain a fair view of the enterprise's performance; to train employees; not to engage in discrimination in their employment practices. The Review added recommendations in relation to those core labour standards that were missing from the earlier text (child labour and forced labour, in particular). In addition, other sections of the Guidelines deal with issues that are relevant to labour standards. For example, they recommend that companies encourage application of the Guidelines within their supply chain.

Since the adoption of the Guidelines, around 30 requests for clarifications – including two since 1996 – have been brought to the CIME, mostly by TUAC, but also by the Belgian, Danish, Dutch and French governments. Since the Committee does not reach conclusions on the conduct of *individual* enterprises, these cases have been raised as requests for "clarification" of the Guidelines. The CIME has issued clarifications in response to questions raised, explaining in more detail the meaning of existing provisions in concrete situations in order to assist the parties concerned when using the Guidelines. Many of these clarifications refer to the provisions of the industrial relations chapter. These have included, for example, issues related to infringements of the right of employees to be represented by trade unions; to the provision of reasonable notice in case of major changes in company operations; and to the provision of information to employee representatives to enable them to obtain a true and fair view of enterprise performance.

Private-sector codes of conduct

Voluntary efforts to define and implement appropriate standards for business conduct constitute one of the more noteworthy trends in international business over the past fifteen years. The issuance of voluntary codes of conduct has been an important facet of this development. Codes of conduct are written expressions of commitment to a given standard of business conduct. They are issued by individual businesses, business associations, non-governmental organisations, governments and inter-governmental organisations. Labour issues are often discussed in these codes. Indeed, a recent survey of the content of over 200 codes ("Codes of Corporate Conduct: An Inventory" [TD/TC/WP(98)74/FINAL]) shows that labour relations and environment are the two most commonly cited issue areas.

Box 8.   **Private codes in the US apparel industry**

The Apparel Industry Partnership (comprising NGOs and US apparel firms) agreed in November 1998 on an industry-wide code aiming at the abolition of sweatshops in the US and abroad. It is supported by a number of major companies. The Partnership includes a workplace code of conduct setting out decent and humane conditions and addressing issues such as forced labour, child labour, harassment, health and safety, freedom of association and collective bargaining, wages and working hours.

A 1996 report "The Apparel Industry and Codes of Conduct: A Solution to the International Child Labor Problem?" by the US Department of Labor's Bureau of International Labor Affairs [USDOL (1996)] focussed on child labour. It highlighted the fact that many US companies importing apparel have adopted codes of conduct prohibiting the use of child labour, among other labour standards. The report concluded that voluntary initiatives, such as codes of conduct, constitute a positive step towards the elimination of child labour. However, it stressed that the monitoring of implementation is essential, in particular for subcontractors.

72

In the US, most Fortune 500 companies have adopted codes of conduct, or some form of internal guidelines, many of which deal with core labour standards. Non US-companies are also adopting such codes or guidelines including Honda, Sony, Siemens, and SmithKline Beecham. In the UK, more than 60% of the top 500 companies have codes of conduct according to estimates made by the Institute of Business Ethics. A decade ago, the figure was 18% (*Financial Times*, 5 August 1999).

Initiatives are taken not only by companies. Codes dealing with labour practices are also being developed unilaterally by business groups and other groups representing public interests or as a result of joint undertakings between trade unions and individual enterprises. Examples include a Code of Conduct regarding the Rights of Workers agreed by IKEA and the International Federation of Building and Woodworkers (IFBWW); and a Code of Conduct agreed between STATOIL and Norsk Olje Petrokjemisk Fagforbund/International Federation of Chemical, Energy, Mine and General Workers.

Recent consultations between the OECD and various business firms and associations highlight several reasons for issuance of codes (and implementation of related management systems). Companies wish: to integrate broader corporate responsibility initiatives with their efforts to comply with laws; to preserve and enhance their corporate reputations as important business assets; to reinforce their ability to compete in tight labour markets and to boost employee morale and loyalty to the firm; and to become eligible for financing from ethical investing funds.

Recent surveys of the labour content of such codes show that the treatment of this issue is as diverse as the organisations issuing the codes [see Diller (2000)]. Among the codes that deal with labour, some of the most commonly mentioned issues are reasonable working environments, child labour, forced labour and working hours. Many of the labour codes focus on relations with suppliers and sub-contractors and, in some cases, business partners are asked to sign the codes.

Corporate codes are often accompanied by measures designed to make them meaningful to the day-to-day operations of the firm. Measures include the creation of compliance offices, internal monitoring, new record-keeping practices (designed to produce data on performance with respect to the commitments), the creation of whistle-blowing facilities and the hiring of external monitoring services. Often these measures take the form of management systems involving record-keeping, operating procedures, training, incentive schemes and corrective actions to be taken in the event of incomplete compliance with the code and reporting and disclosure practices.

The growth in the number of corporate codes has occurred in such an *ad hoc* fashion that it is difficult to determine the scope and implications of this trend.

Box 9. Codes of conduct in the EU

A code of conduct was adopted in September 1997 by the social partners in the European textile and clothing sector [European Apparel and Textile Organisation (EURATEX) for the employers and European Trade Union Federation of Textiles, Clothing and Leather (ETUF/TCL) for the workers]. It includes provisions relating to forced labour, freedom of association and the right to negotiate, child labour and non-discrimination in employment. Through the inclusion of clauses in national collective agreements, the content of this code acquires legal status and binding force. It therefore constitutes an interesting example of how problems related to implementation and monitoring of codes of conduct can be tackled.

The social partners in the European footwear sector [European Confederation of the footwear Industry (CEC) for the employers and European Trade Union Federation of Textiles, Clothing and Leather (ETUF/TCL) for the workers] adopted in 1995 a charter on child labour which they revised in 1997. Thanks to a recent agreement with the European Confederation of the Shoe Retailers Association (CEDDEC), representing the European shoe retailers, the charter has been significantly extended. The social partners in the European tanning industry [Confederation of National Associations of Tanners and Dressers of the European Community] (COTANCE) and ETUF/TCL agreed a code of conduct in March 2000 that covers core labour standards as set out in the relevant ILO Conventions.

EuroCommerce and Euro-FIET, representing the employers and the workers in European commerce respectively, adopted in March 1996 a joint statement on combating child labour. EuroCommerce and Euro-FIET concluded an Agreement on fundamental principles and rights at work in 1999 on the basis of the June 1998 ILO Declaration.

The International Federation of Building and Wood Workers (IFBWW) has been working with enterprises to seek effective implementation of all core ILO Conventions. It signed agreements with IKEA in May 1998, Faber-Castell in March 2000 and Hochtief in March 2000. The agreement with Hochtief imposes the same conditions on the company's sub-contractors.

The Initiative for Ethical Consumption and Production in Europe (IEPCE) was launched in December 1999, with support from the European Commission. IEPCE is a forum for companies, employers' associations, trade unions, NGO's, experts and public authorities. Its first objective is to structure and exchange existing information on initiatives related to ethical production and consumption such as codes of conduct and social labels.

The Ethical Trading Initiative (ETI) is a UK initiative based on co-operation between industry, NGOs, trade unions and government, which has been operational since mid-1998. It is funded by company membership fees, NGOs and a grant from the UK Department for International Development. It has developed a code based on ILO conventions, containing 9 principles: no forced labour, freedom of association and the right to collective bargaining, safe and hygienic working conditions, no use of child workers, living wages, limits to working hours, non-discrimination, regularity of employment and no harsh or inhumane treatment. ETI is also implementing a programme of pilot studies. Currently underway are studies on clothing in China, wine in South Africa, horticulture in Zimbabwe and Zambia and bananas in Costa Rica. Member companies are committed to the adoption of the "ETI base code", to participate in pilot studies with other members and to provide an annual report. Membership is on an annual basis and may not be renewed for members not demonstrating commitment to the ETI process.

There is no registry of codes. Only recently have different organisations, including the OECD, launched projects to collect and analyse corporate codes. Future work of OECD in this area will seek to clarify some of the issues that arise: *e.g.* the significance of codes in economic activity, including trade; how codes work; and whether they are effective in achieving their objectives. This work also underpinned the recent review of the OECD Guidelines (see above).

The creation of standardised management systems is a noteworthy development in this area, though there is less agreement in the business community about standards for labour management than about some other areas (*e.g.* ISO 14001 is a widely-accepted environmental management system). Social Accountability 8000 (SA 8000) is a management standard in the labour area. SA 8000 is intended to strengthen workplace codes by addressing definitions and concepts that can facilitate the "auditability" and monitoring of codes (see Council on Economic Priorities *www.cepaa.org*, 1999).

Global Compact

At the World Economic Forum, in Davos, on 31 January 1999, UN Secretary General, Kofi Annan, called on world business to initiate a Global Compact of shared values and principles, which will give a human face to the global market.[42] The Compact's nine principles include commitments on human rights, labour and environment. Those based on the fundamental principles and rights of the 1998 ILO Declaration, are: the freedom of association and the effective recognition of the right to collective bargaining, the elimination of all forms of forced and compulsory labour, the effective abolition of child labour, and the elimination of discrimination in respect of employment and occupation.

Private-party mechanisms

Some associations campaign through their websites for the improvement of working conditions in developing countries and call on consumers to boycott the products of companies which allegedly do not respect workers' rights (see Box 10).

Labelling of consumer goods

In 1998, the ILO issued a study on the role of labelling initiatives in the attempt to eliminate or ameliorate the problem of child labour.[43] In addition to Rugmark carpet labelling (examined in the 1996 study), the ILO Study reviews four labelling initiatives targeting child labour in the sector of hand-knotted carpets: the Kaleen Label for carpets, the Care and Fare label, the Step Label for carpet, and the Abrinq Labelling initiative; and the double income project in the textile and cloth manufacturing sectors (see Box 11).

75

Box 10. **Moral suasion**

This brief update draws on material recently obtained from the Internet. For instance, Labour Behind the Label[1] campaigns for the improvement of garment workers' working conditions and calls on retailers to take responsibility for working conditions at all stages of the production. This network includes a number of organisations.[2] Labour Behind the Label encourages retailers to adopt codes of conduct respecting the core conventions set by the ILO and guaranteeing good working conditions, a living wage and the right to join independent trade unions to all workers involved in the product chain, accept independent verification of how codes are put into place and make such information available to consumers. On its website, the organisation encourages consumers to support workers who make clothes by sending post cards to a range of companies.

Other websites promoting working conditions and encouraging consumers to boycott companies who allegedly do not respect workers' rights include Corpwatch,[3] The Maquila Solidarity Network,[4] Global Exchange,[5] Ropalimpia,[6] and Solidarmonde.[7]

1. *http://www.traidcraft.co.uk/labour.htm.*
2. CAFOD, Central America Women Network, Ethical Consumer, Jacob's Well, KFAT, National Group on Home working, NEAD, Tradcraft Exchange, Women Working Worldwide, World Development Movement.
3. *http://www.corpwatch.org/trac/nike/.*
    http://www.corpwatch.org/trac/corner/alert/toys-r-us.html.
4. *http://www.web.net/~msn/2aboutus.htm.*
5. *http://www.globalexchange.org/economy/corporations/.*
6. *http://www.panfgea.org/ropalimpia/equeesla.htm.*
7. *http://www.solidarmonde.fr.*

The study identifies four common features among social labelling initiatives: the use of a physical label on the product or by a retail establishment; outreach to consumers; oversight; and a levy on the product paid by the retailer or importer. It also noted differences among the schemes under review including: the application of a label to a specific product or to an establishment; the internal or external conduct of monitoring and oversight; and a difference in goals ranging from the total elimination of child labour from any production role to the improvement of working conditions for children.

Other international labelling initiatives include International Fairtrade Labelling,[44] which encompasses labelling initiatives in 17 countries,[45] mainly in Europe and North America, for a range of products: coffee, chocolate, orange juice, tea, honey, sugar and bananas. The aim of the Fairtrade Labelling Organisations (FLOs) is to

Box 11.   **Recent labelling initiatives**

The *Kaleen Label* for carpets is an initiative of the Indian Government, which decided in mid-1995 through its Carpet Export Promotion Council (CEPC) to create its own carpet-labelling programme. In August 1996, the Ministry of Commerce issued a ruling making it mandatory for all carpet exporters to become members of the CEPC. The blanket requirement for membership is adherence to an anti-child labour "voluntary code" and the contribution of 0.25% of all carpet export earnings to a special fund for improving the welfare of children in the rural carpet-weaving communities. The Kaleen initiative depends upon self-regulation by the carpet industry though the CEPC, monitored by an appointed government committee of experts.

Initiated in 1994, *Care and Fair Label* responds to the desire of many German carpet importers and retailers to create better living prospects for children and their families in the carpet-making regions of India and Nepal. The Care and Fair charter consists of nine commitments including stipulations regarding child labour. Care and Fair does not itself directly engage in any monitoring or inspection of work sites. It collects a levy of between one and two per cent of the carpet import value per square meter from its membership in order to finance projects in the carpet-producers area. Members also pay a yearly fee of DM 250.

The STEP *Label* is the creation of a small Swiss foundation which licenses retailer carpet dealers in Switzerland to use it in their stores. It also undertakes some monitoring and inspection of production sites in India and Nepal. The contract contains a six-point Code of Conduct, including the rejection of the use of child labour. Licensees pay the STEP foundation a fixed sum per square meter of carpet sold.

The *Abrinq* Foundation set up a labelling initiative designed to encourage child-friendly companies and provide labelling for their products. Abrinq offers child-friendly labels to companies that do not employ child labour and that also contribute to child development. Abrinq's activities have received support from the ILO, UNICEF and other national and international organisations and foundations as well as from a number of Brazilian companies. The "Child-Friendly Enterprise" Programme has two aims: *i)* to mobilise entrepreneurial commitment to avoid using child labour; and *ii)* to increase the level of company support for helping children to attend school, vocational or professional training. It also promotes the inclusion of a social clause in commercial contracts, so that companies make a commitment to combating child labour. The labelling programme is monitored and companies are inspected each year before renewal of their right to use the label.

The *Double Income Project* (DIP) based in Switzerland was founded in 1995. It provides labelling for textiles and garments imported into Switzerland from developing countries. Labelled products must be produced in a socially acceptable manner and without child labour. The companies must comply with national laws (*e.g.* regarding minimum wages, working age, etc) and with the Ecotex standard for environmentally-safe production. DIP expects its textile and clothing manufacturer licensees to "double" the wages of their workers and donate the second part directly to the project, which is then invested in various welfare projects for the workers' benefit. The bulk of production is imported into Switzerland and for each labelled product imported, the Swiss importer also pays one US dollar to the DIP joint-venture project. DIP therefore collects from both the producer and the importer. DIP has licensed factories in India and Kenya (textile and garment manufacturers), but has also certified some jewellery and handicraft manufactures in South America.

contribute to an increased control by developing countries' producers over their own production to guarantee continuity of income and decent working and living conditions.

The FLO criteria are individually researched for each Fairtrade labelled product, in consultation with the producers and workers concerned, in order to reflect the differences between each product. Besides fair trading conditions,[46] the Fairtrade label seeks to guarantee fair production conditions. These include a democratic, participative structure for small farmers' co-operatives; for plantations and factories they include: decent wages (at least the legal minimum), good housing where appropriate, minimum health and safety standards, the right to join trade unions, no child or forced labour, and minimum environmental requirement. The FLO monitoring programme ensures that all the trading partners continue to comply with Fairtrade criteria. The framework for bananas and orange juice directly refers to compliance with ILO Conventions. The framework for tea lists a range of core labour standards without referring expressly to the ILO Conventions. The "fair conditions" for honey and sugar, cocoa and coffee only mention non-discrimination, integral social development, the creation of better living conditions and integral human participation.

Notwithstanding limitations which critics ascribe to labelling (see Part II), the US Department of Labor referred, in its 1997 report on *Sweat and Toil of Children*, to the effectiveness of voluntary labelling in preventing international use of child labour in the production of hand-knotted carpets, leather footwear, soccer balls and tea. In addition to reducing child labour in targeted industries, some labelling programmes, it is reported, raise funds for educational and rehabilitation programmes for former child workers.

Socially responsible investing

According to the Social Investment Organisation, a Canadian non-profit organisation committed to the development of socially responsible investment (SRI), in the past 30 years, investors have become more systematic in applying non-monetary, value-based criteria to their investments.[47] SRI involves investors directing their investment capital for both financial return and progressive social change. The underlying mechanism is to "screen" companies for whether or not their policies or practices meet certain social and environmental performance criteria. Screening can also take place based on other ethical or moral concerns, such as whether the activities of a company involve alcohol, tobacco or gambling or promote political objectives such as peace and democracy. Social investors include not only individuals but also businesses, universities, hospitals, foundations, pension funds, religious institutions and other non-profit organisations.[48]

While SRI was popular in the past with investors who did not want their investments to support the Vietnam War or South Africa's apartheid system, interest among investors and financial institutions has grown significantly, especially during the past decade.

According to available figures, the number of mutual and money market funds in the United States that used some type of social screening increased from about a half a dozen in the early 1980s to over 60 by 1995. There were 44 ethical trusts and funds in the United Kingdom in 1996. In Canada, 18 mutual funds employed social and/or environmental criteria in 1999. In the case of the United States, more than $2 trillion was invested in late 1999 in a socially responsible manner, up 82% from 1997 levels, according to a study released in November 1999 by the Social Investment Forum. This figure includes all segments of social investing (screened portfolios, shareholders advocacy and community investing) and accounts for roughly 13% of the $16.3 trillion in investment assets under professional management in the US. The Forum's 1999 report on Socially Responsible Investing Trends in the US stresses the rapid growth of the socially screened portfolios (a 183% increase). While tobacco remains the principal concern for social investors (96%), the labour issue was a concern for some 38%.

SRI can also involve shareholding activism: shareholders promoting actively their values by criticising the policies and practices of those corporations in which they hold shares. For example, it has become more common for shareholders to sponsor or co-sponsor resolutions challenging a company to bring its practices and policies in line with their views about social issues.

Concluding remarks

Since the 1996 study was completed there has been a strengthening of some mechanisms to promote core labour standards world-wide, for example:

- Systems for promoting, monitoring and enforcing the ILO conventions have become stronger, in part, through increased numbers of ratifications and through specific follow-up to the ILO Declaration. But there remains a twin challenge for the ILO: to get key information to users where it can do the most good in a timely fashion; and to focus international attention on the most serious infractions in a way that leads to early improvements.

- The contribution of development co-operation programmes in eradicating exploitative forms of child labour has become more focussed and results-oriented.

Other bilateral and multilateral mechanisms – such as the North American Agreement on Labor Cooperation, at the regional level, and the US and EC GSP schemes at the national level – continue to be used effectively on a selective basis. In addition, some private sector mechanisms – such as codes of conduct, various labelling initiatives and socially responsible investing – appear to be attracting widening interest and participation.

It is too soon to assess the overall impact of the post-1996 developments on the promotion of – and respect for – core labour standards. Nevertheless, there is some evidence of positive results from the workings of these types of mechanisms (*e.g.*, reports from ILO experts that the ILO supervisory systems have led to improvements concerning forced labour in certain countries or ICFTU observers who note that the US GSP Program has led to increased respect for freedom of association in certain regions). And, there is a tendency toward expanded coverage and increased focus of the various mechanisms.

Notes

1. In the case of ILO conventions, according to the constitution of the organisation (Article 19(5)(d)), ILO members ratifying a convention "will take such action as may be necessary to make effective the provisions of such convention". The ILO Handbook (4, III) notes that, in order to be registered, an instrument of ratification must "clearly convey the Government's intention that the State should be bound by the Convention concerned and its undertaking to fulfil the Convention's provisions...". Moreover, while ILO conventions are not enforced through sanctions, a country that fails to honour the fundamental principles embodied in the ILO's fundamental conventions may still risk adverse action. For example, it may lose incentives under bilateral or international agreements (*e.g.*, under the US or EU GSP programmes) or it may face a loss of foreign assistance. (Also, see Part III for a detailed discussion of promotion mechanisms.)

2. While there were no opposing votes, it should be acknowledged that some countries demonstrated reticence toward the ILO Declaration by abstaining. The final vote was 273 in favour, none opposing and 43 abstentions. A quorum of 264 was necessary for the motion to pass.

3. Decisions on those priorities are taken by the ILO Governing Body, which then adopts action plans to address the issues. The follow-up to the ILO Declaration is discussed in more detail in Part III of this report.

4. The Programme of Action refers to "basic workers' rights, including prohibition of forced labour and child labour, freedom of association and the right to organise and bargain collectively, equal remuneration for men and women for work of equal value and non-discrimination in employment..." (Programme of Action, Item C, Paragraph 54(*b*), quoted from the Summit's Internet site at *http://www.un.org/esa/socdev/wssd/agreements/*).

5. Specifically, for the purposes of analysis, the 1996 study defined four core labour standards as being embodied in five ILO conventions (shown in brackets) including: *i*) the freedom of association and right to collective bargaining [Conventions 87 and 98]; *ii*) elimination of exploitative forms of child labour; *iii*) prohibition of forced labour [Conventions 29 and 105]; and *iv*) non-discrimination in employment [Convention 111].

6. Convention No. 138 permits several exceptions to this minimum, such as for countries "whose economy and educational facilities are insufficiently developed" which may initially specify a minimum age of 14 years after consulting with the social partners. Also, it should be noted that many countries are bound by minimum age restrictions in one or more of the 10 sectoral conventions that predate Convention No. 138.

7. Certain conventions provide for exclusions, exceptions or options, sometimes requiring ratifying countries to declare their situation at the time of ratification. E.g., countries have flexibility under Article 2 of the Minimum Age Convention (No. 138) to specify their own minimum age requirements for workers within the parameters laid out in the convention.

8. Information concerning the application of ILO conventions was drawn primarily from ILO (1999*b*) and ILO (1999*f*). For a detailed list of sources, see Annex Table A.2.

9. Hong Kong, China, is listed separately in the tables but is not included in the various country counts.

10. The United States has also ratified Convention 182, which is to become a fundamental convention effective November 2000.

11. For example, the CEACR has maintained that the ban on the right to strike for public servants in Germany is too broad, a point the government disputes.

12. ILO (1999*f*), pp. 204-206. This point remains under discussion with the government.

13. ILO (1999*b*), CEACR individual observation for Australia, Convention 98, Document No. 061998AUS098, Section 4. This point remains under discussion with the government.

14. ILO (1999*b*), CEACR individual observation for the United Kingdom, Convention 98, Document No. 061996GBR0982, Section 1.

15. Brown, D.K. (forthcoming), *International Trade and Core Labour Standards: A Survey of The Recent Literature*, Labour Market and Social Policy Occasional Papers, OECD, Paris.

16. Other analysis, however, suggests that education and work are not necessarily incompatible. Patrinos and Psacharopoulos (1997), examining the case of Peru, find that child labour makes it possible for children to attend school, and that part-time work and schooling can be complementary.

17. The OECD 1996 study also points out that no single pattern holds for all countries and that in eight of the seventeen countries examined GDP growth fell after the improvement in freedom of association.

18. Kuruvilla (1996), based on the experiences of Singapore, Malaysia, the Philippines and India, shows that labour rights are negatively correlated with a successful export promotion strategy.

19. The Stolper-Samuelson theorem suggests that an increase in trade through the removal of import barriers will raise the real return of the factor used relatively intensively in the production of exports.

20. The countries included in the analysis were Australia, Canada, Denmark, Finland, Germany, Japan, Sweden, the United Kingdom and the United States.

21. Basu (1999) points out that detailed empirical work would have to be undertaken in order to be certain that a ban on child labour would, in fact, force a high-wage/no child labour equilibrium to emerge.

22. In commenting on the limitations of labelling schemes, Palley (1999) refers to costs of implementation and difficulties of verification. He also suggests there is an ethical question insofar as labelling can put the economic well-being of workers in developing countries in the hands of consumers in developed countries.

23. As noted below, the ILO Declaration includes a provision for annual reports by ILO Member countries that have not ratified fundamental conventions. This follow-up procedure, however, is not considered to be part of the ILO supervision of conventions but rather a distinct promotional mechanism.

24. The CEACR annual reports from 1995 to 1999 (inclusive) included expressions of satisfaction in an average of 34 cases per year, while the average number of individual country observations was 457.

25. There is an important complementary action between the CEACR and the CFA. The CEACR monitoring systematically captures information reported by the government and garnered through comments from employers and workers organisations; the CFA mechanism is complaints-driven and brings into focus problems related to freedom of association in a more expedited fashion.

26. For example, in correspondence with the OECD, the ILO secretariat provided information on a recent internal study by the Freedom of Association Branch concerning Conventions 87 and 98. That study described 134 cases of progress identified by the CEACR with respect to these two conventions between 1970 and 1996. The annual average number of such cases increased from a level of about 3 per year in the 1970s and 1980s to nearly 10 per year during 1990-96.

27. Under the regular system of supervision, the staggered scheduling of country reports on conventions leads to variations in the number of CEACR observations; there are "on" years and "off" years for each convention depending on its particular schedule for submission of reports to the CEACR. Convention 29, for example, is examined in even years and Convention 105 in odd years.

28. China has not ratified the two forced labour conventions and is not considered here.

29. Article 33 of the ILO Constitution states that, "In the event of any Member failing to carry out within the time specified the recommendations, if any, contained in the report of the Commission of Inquiry, or in the decision of the International Court of Justice, as the case may be, the Governing Body may recommend to the Conference such action as it may deem wise and expedient to secure compliance therewith". Additional information on this case is available in an ILO press release dated 14 June 2000. See: *http://www.ilo.org/public/english/bureau/inf/pr/2000/27.htm.*

30. A late report was subsequently submitted by Pakistan bringing the total to 15 as of mid-May 2000.

31. In the case of the effective abolition of child labour, just over one-half of all ILO member countries were requested to submit reports. With respect to the other categories of fundamental principles and rights, less than one-third of ILO member states were requested to submit reports. Despite the large number of ILO members excluded from the reporting requirements, countries failing to submit requested reports nevertheless accounted for substantial shares of ILO membership. With respect to the effective abolition of child labour, the number of countries failing to report amounted to 25 per cent of the ILO membership. With respect to the other categories of principles and rights, the failure to report concerned about ten per cent of ILO member states.

32. Available at: *http://www.ilo.org/public/english/20gb/docs/gb276/sdl-1.htm#Synthesis.*

33. Reference is made to ILO Convention 182 on the Worst Forms of Child Labour for a listing of the types of child labour concerned, including all forms of slavery or practices similar to slavery, forced or compulsory labour, sexual exploitation, illicit activities and work likely to harm the health, safety or morals of children.

34. *http://wbln0018.worldbank.org/HDNet/HD.nsf/SectorPages.*

35. The AFL-CIO remains the most frequent petitioner followed by International Labour Rights Fund (formerly the International Labor Rights Education and Research Fund) and Human Rights Watch, although any interested party is permitted to file a petition, including individuals and small interest groups.

36. Council Regulation No. 03281/94, OJ L 348.

37. Council Regulation (EC) No. 2820/98 of 21 December 1998 applying a multiannual scheme of generalised tariff preferences for the period 1 July 1999 to 31 December 2001, OJ L357 of December 1998, pp.1-112).

38. The modulation mechanism applies both to agricultural and industrial products listed in annexes. For agricultural products, preferential duty shall be reduced by an amount ranging between minus 10% and minus 35% of the Common Customs Tariff duty; for industrial products, the additional preferential margin ranges between minus 15% and minus 35% of the Common Customs Tariff duties. Moreover, graduated products can benefit from an additional incentive provision of 15% for agricultural products and of 25% for industrial products.

39. Notice of the Commission C 176, OJ C 176 of 22.6.1999, p. 13.

40. Notice of the Commission C 218, OJ C 218 of 30.7.1999, p. 2.

41. Council Regulation (EC) No. 552/97 of 24 March 1997 temporarily withdrawing access to generalised tariff preferences from the Union of Myanmar, OJ L 085 of 27 March 1997 p. 8.

42. Secretary-General Proposes Global Compact on Human Rights, Labour, Environment, in address to World Economic Forum in Davos, Press Release SG/SM/6881, *www.un.org/ news/press/docs/*1999.

43. *http://www.ilo.org/public/englsh/90ipec/publ/lapred/*.

44. *http://www.fairtrade.net*.

45. The first initiative was launched in the Netherlands in 1998, with the Max Havelaar label. This label is now used in Belgium, Switzerland, France, Denmark and Norway. Other labels include FairTrade (Ireland, UK, Austria, Canada, Germany, Italy, Japan, Luxembourg and USA) and Rätvisenmärkt (Sweden).

46. Fair Trading relations include: a price that covers the cost of production, social premium for development purposes, partial payment in advance to avoid small producers falling into debt, contracts that allow long-term production planning, long-term trade relations that allow proper planning and sustainable production practices.

47. *www.web.net/~sio/history.htm*.

48. Rory O'Brien: "Overview of the Field of Socially Responsible Investing (SRI)". *http:// web.net/~robien/papers/sri/srioview.htm*.

A Review of CEACR Observations Concerning ILO Conventions 87 and 98

The ILO does not monitor overall progress in cases of non-compliance identified by the CEACR against a standard overall benchmark (*e.g.*, the number and severity of cases outstanding). In order to provide an estimate, the OECD Secretariat developed a non-compliance indicator based on earlier work on the Index of Compliance outlined in the Annex to the OECD's 1996 study.

The OECD Secretariat reviewed published observations from the CEACR concerning ILO Conventions 87 and 98 during the period from 1989 to 1999 using data from the ILOLEX database [ILO(1999*b*)]. Earlier years were not included in the Secretariat review due to their limited coverage in ILOLEX. The OECD review covered the 69 countries listed in Table 2 of the present update that had ratifications in effect for either Convention 87 or Convention 98 during this period.* This limitation was imposed because the CEACR only reports on countries that have ratified a given convention. The original methodology from the 1996 study was modified in order to produce a score adjusted to take into account the number of ratifications in effect for the two conventions in each year for the 69 countries.

The review found a total of 1289 cases of non-compliance identified by the CEACR in published observations concerning the two conventions during the period. It should be kept in mind that some countries had more than one case of non-compliance in a given year (*e.g.*, with respect to the right to strike and the right to establish free unions). The number of cases fluctuated from year to year as new cases arose or the CEACR expressed satisfaction at the resolution of outstanding issues. A general review of these cases indicates that, between 1989 and 1999, the volume varied widely from a low of 56 in 1990 to a high of 164 in 1999. Perhaps more indicative of the frequency of non-compliance among countries, is the number of cases identified by the CEACR for each country that had ratified a convention. This statistic ranged from a low of 0.5 cases per country per ratified convention in 1990 to a high of 1.5 in 1991 (partly due to consideration of late submissions from 1990), with the other years falling between 0.8 and 1.3 findings.

As in the 1996 study, the Secretariat developed a non-compliance score for each case identified by the CEACR. The score consists of two parts. First, each case was assigned a rating based on the type and degree of restriction identified by the CEACR with respect to freedom of association or the right to organise and bargain collectively (A). Then, a second rating was assigned based on the CEACR's evaluation of the situation and required remedy (B). The rating system was essentially the same one used in the 1996 study. Once the

---

* Eight countries shown in Table 2 did not have ratifications for either convention in effect during the period from 1989 to 1999: Chile, China, India, Iran, Thailand, Korea, New Zealand and the United States. Chile ratified both conventions in 1999 but these ratifications had not yet come into effect at the time of this review.

ratings were assigned, each case was then scored by multiplying the two ratings (A times B). The scores for each case could range from 0 (full compliance) to 20 (extreme non-compliance). Over time, the score for a given case could fluctuate upwards or downwards depending on changes in the situation as evaluated by the CEACR.

The case scores were summed for each year across all of the ratifying countries. This sum was divided by the number of ratifying countries in order to produce an annual average country score per ratified convention that takes into account the number and severity of outstanding cases.

Thus, for example, if there was a single case of non-compliance identified by the CEACR in an individual country, a score was assigned. If over time there was progress or the CEACR ceased to identify a problem in that country, then the score was reduced or eliminated. Progress was reflected in an improved score for that country (*i.e.*, one that moved closer to 0 (compliance) and away from 20 (non-compliance)). The index is an average of all the scores in a given year for each convention taking into account cases of progress, lack of progress and worsening in compliance as reported formally by the CEACR with respect to countries that have ratified the conventions.

The non-compliance indicator can be represented as:

Non-compliance indicator $_t$ = $\Sigma_c \Sigma_i [A_{ict} \times B_{ict}]$ / (number of country ratifications in effect).

Where:

A *is rating of the nature of the case, ranging from 5 to 1:*

5 = most severe type of violation (*e.g.*, violent intimidation of union members);

4 = severe violation (*e.g.*, prohibition of union activity or collective bargaining);

3 = major restriction (*e.g.*, wrongful denial of right to organise or bargain collectively in certain sectors or for certain categories of workers);

2 = moderately severe restriction (*e.g.*, eligibility requirements for union leaders);

1 = least severe restriction (*e.g.*, prohibition of political activity of unions).

B *is rating of the* CEACR *evaluation of the situation and remedy, ranging from 4 to 0:*

4 = most critical CEACR evaluation (*e.g.*, situation is inconsistent with ILO requirements; no government response);

3 = critical evaluation (*e.g.*, situation is inconsistent with ILO requirements; government is amending labour laws);

2 = moderately critical evaluation (*e.g.*, labour law amended; information requested on enforcement);

1 = least critical evaluation (*e.g.*, labour law amended and enforcement is improving; further information requested);

0 = favourable evaluation (*e.g.*, situation is consistent with ILO requirements).

i = CEACR findings concerning ILO conventions 87 and 98, as documented in the published individual country observations;

c = countries that had ratified a given convention by the point in time under consideration;

t = year, ranging from 1989 through 1999.

Notes: *a*) Each country may have up to two ratifications in effect, one for each convention; *b*) The CEACR schedules reviews of country reports on Convention 87 for odd-numbered years and reviews of Convention 98 for even-numbered years.

For a variety of reasons, the non-compliance indicator provides only an approximate measure of the application of conventions, as assessed through the CEACR monitoring mechanism. First, although the CEACR schedules reporting requirements for the two conventions on alternate years, there is some slippage. Due to late submissions, some reports are considered in the subsequent years. Convention 87 years include some Convention 98 cases and *vice versa*. Second, countries may send incomplete responses that result in delays in the CEACR ability to assess the case. Third, in some cases the CEACR simply repeats its previous years' evaluation, but the use of such repetitions may not be done in a uniform manner across all countries and over time. Fourth, there may be variation across countries and across years in the CEACR's stringency. Fifth, the assignment of ratings depends on an element of OECD Secretariat judgement. (However, the CEACR's use of roughly standardised language across countries and over time helps to reduce inconsistencies in these judgements.)

The non-compliance indicator covering all 69 countries is shown in Chart A.1, Panel 1. The higher the score shown, the greater the average degree of non-compliance identified in the CEACR observations. The low score in 1990 and high score in 1991 are partly due to a high number of late submissions in 1990, which were probably considered in the following year. For this reason, it may be appropriate to exclude 1990-91 from any trend assessments. Comparing 1989 and 1993 (Convention 87 years) and 1992 (a Convention 98 year) with corresponding years later in the decade, reveals a modest increase in the scores.

In order to clarify the picture, the Secretariat adjusted the CEACR findings to remove observations repeated or restated in two consecutive years and to assign late CEACR observations to the year intended for the review of the convention in question. The results are presented in Panel 2. This adjustment smoothes the fluctuation in scores during the early 1990s and reduces the average scores somewhat. The chart reveals a slight tendency toward improvement in the average CEACR observation concerning Convention 87. A worsening of scores with respect to Convention 98 is still evident between the first and second halves of the decade.

These results must be interpreted with care, keeping in mind the caveats mentioned above and recalling that the indicator depends on CEACR commentary on reporting gleaned through the ILO supervisory systems rather than direct observation of the situation in the field. Nevertheless, the indicator does show a significant degree of continuing non-compliance among countries that have ratified the two conventions in question. It is also disturbing that, despite the increased international political consensus with respect to core labour standards during the decade, there is no clear indication of substantial progress overall in reducing non-compliance with respect to these two conventions. The results also highlight difficulties in the operation of the ILO supervisory systems, whereby many country reports are submitted late and where the CEACR is moved to repeat or recall concerns from year to year.

Chart A.1.   **Index of non-compliance for ILO Conventions 87 and 98, 1989-1999**
OECD Secretariat assessment of CEACR observations covering 69 countries

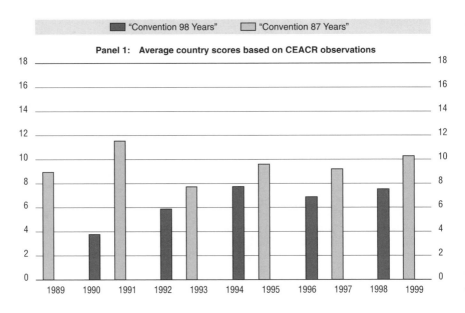

Panel 1:   **Average country scores based on CEACR observations**

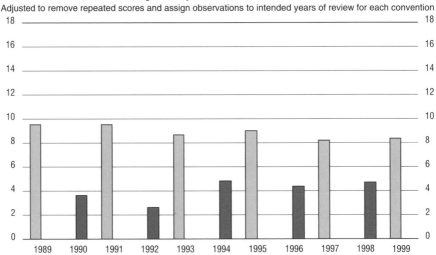

Panel 2:   **Average country scores based on CEACR observations**
Adjusted to remove repeated scores and assign observations to intended years of review for each convention

Sources: ILOLEX database and OECD Secretariat assessments and calculations.

Table A.1. **Basic economic indicators**

	Per capita GDP (US$) (1995)[a]	Growth in real per capita GDP (1985-90)	Growth in real per capita GDP (1990-95)	Exports, f.o.b. (US$ billion) (1995)
Non-OECD				
Argentina	8 042	−2.2	5.2	21.0
Bahamas	12 409	0.2	−2.1	0.2
Bangladesh	246	1.7	2.6	3.2
Barbados	6 678	3.6	−0.4	0.2
Bolivia	827	0.3	1.3	1.1
Botswana	2 978	7.2	1.6	2.1
Brazil	4 327	0.0	1.4	46.5
Chile	4 736	5.1	5.6	16.1
China	585	6.6	11.6	148.8
Chinese Taipei	12 266	7.9	5.3	111.6
Colombia	2 260	2.4	2.7	10.1
Ecuador	1 562	−0.3	1.1	4.3
Egypt	762	0.5	−0.7	3.4
Ethiopia	98	1.9	2.5[b]	0.4
Fiji	2 640	2.5	1.2	0.6
Guatemala	1 365	0.2	1.3	2.2
Haiti	286	−1.7	−8.3	0.1
Honduras	697	0.5	0.6	1.1
Hong Kong, China	22 908	6.7	4.1	173.8
India	349	4.5	2.8	30.7
Indonesia	1 003	4.3	5.4	45.4
Iran	1 561	−5.7	1.1	18.4
Israel	15 698	2.1	2.8	19.0
Jamaica	1 787	4.6	0.2	1.4
Jordan	1 237	−3.9	3.1	17.7
Kenya	326	2.2	−1.6	1.9
Kuwait	15 731	−3.4	16.5	12.9
Malaysia	4 235	4.2	6.1	74.0
Malta	8 744	5.8	4.6	1.9
Mauritius	3 511	6.7	3.8	1.5
Morocco	1 222	2.1	−0.8	4.6
Niger	203	−1.6	−2.8	0.3
Pakistan	433	2.6	1.8	8.0
Panama	2 816	−4.1	3.5	0.6
Papua New Guinea	1 139	−1.0	6.8	2.7
Peru	2 507	−4.5	3.7	5.6
Philippines	1 094	2.9	0	17.5
Singapore	25 156	6.7	6.6	118.3
South Africa	3 280	−0.3	−1.5	27.9
Sri Lanka	720	1.7	3.8	3.8
Suriname	785	−0.1	−0.3	0.5
Swaziland	1 249	2.3	−0.6	1.0
Syria	3 461	−1.7	4.5	4.0

© OECD 2000

Table A.1. **Basic economic indicators** (*cont.*)

	Per capita GDP (US$) (1995)[a]	Growth in real per capita GDP (1985-90)	Growth in real per capita GDP (1990-95)	Exports, f.o.b. (US$ billion) (1995)
Tanzania	120	0.8	0.6	0.6
Thailand	2 867	9.0	7.4	56.5
Uruguay	5 587	2.9	3.5	2.1
Venezuela	3 496	0.0	0.3	18.5
Zambia	408	−0.5	−2.5	1.2
Zimbabwe	583	0.6	−2.1	2.1
OECD				
Australia	19 517	1.8	2.0	52.7
Austria	29 003	2.7	0.8	57.6
Belgium	26 581	3.1	0.7	171.2[c]
Canada	19 047	1.8	0.6	192.2
Czech Republic[d]	4 365	1.2	−2.5	21.7
Denmark	33 174	1.1	1.7	49.4
Finland	24 473	3.5	−1.1	39.6
France	26 463	2.6	0.4	286.7
Germany	29 567	2.5	1.0	523.8
Greece	10 937	1.6	0.9	11.0
Hungary	4 324	2.7	−1.3	12.5
Iceland	26 216	1.9	−0.4	1.8
Ireland	18 146	5.2	5.2	44.3
Italy	19 005	3.0	0.8	234.0
Japan	40 889	4.3	0.9	443.1
Korea	10 162	9.1	6.2	125.1
Luxembourg	42 565	6.0	4.2	[c]
Mexico	3 147	0.0	0.2	79.5
Netherlands	25 544	2.4	1.1	196.3
New Zealand	16 777	−0.3	2.1	13.7
Norway	33 740	1.0	3.2	42.0
Poland	3 060	−0.1	2.4	22.9
Portugal	9 849	5.2	1.4	22.6
Spain	14 122	4.3	0.9	91.7
Sweden	26 240	1.9	−0.3	79.8
Switzerland	42 719	1.9	−1.0	78.0
Turkey	2 835	3.5	1.9	21.6
United Kingdom	18 971	3.2	1.2	242.0
United States	26 037	1.9	1.6	584.7
World	4 998			5 112.9

a) Current US dollars.
b) 1992-95.
c) Includes Luxembourg.
d) GDP per capita growth between 1985-90 indicates former Czechoslovakia.
Source: UNCTAD, (1999*b*).

Table A.2. **Restrictions on the right to establish free unions**[a, b]

Non-OECD	
Argentina	1996: Only one organisation can be granted representative status at the enterprise level. Bargaining rights and fiscal privileges are accorded only to representative organisations. Update: Most unions remain affiliated with the General Confederation of Labor (CGT) but in 1997 the Government granted legal recognition to a smaller federation, the Central Association of Argentine Workers (CTA).
Bahamas	1996: requirements consistent with ILO conventions. Update: No substantial change noted.
Bangladesh	1996: Professional and industry unions are prohibited in export processing zones. Update: No substantial changes noted. [The CEACR commented on several restrictions in Bangladesh that are not in conformity with the requirements of ILO Convention 87 (e.g., the exclusion of managerial and administrative employees from right of association, restrictions on rights of association of public servants, and excessive external supervision of internal affairs of trade unions). The CFA (Case No. 1862) also raised concerns about several restrictions on union registration that were not in conformity with the Convention (such as a requirement that the union represent 30% of employment at covered establishment(s)).]
Barbados	1996: requirements consistent with ILO conventions. Update: No substantial changes noted.
Bolivia	1996: Only one union can be granted legal status at the enterprise level. Authorities can de-register unions, but rarely do so. Update: No substantial changes noted with respect to the above-mentioned issues. However, previously, agricultural workers were excluded from protections under labour law covering the right to organise. Apparently, these protections were formally extended to wage-earning agricultural workers in December 1996. The CEACR commented that the right to organise should be extended to self-employed rural workers. [Also, under Bolivian labour law, public servants are denied the right to organise.]
Botswana	1996: Union officials must work full-time in the industry they represent. Update: No substantial changes noted. [Workers are generally free to join associations or unions of their choosing, with the exception that government employees may not join unions.]
Brazil	1996: According to the system of "unicidade", no more than one union for the same professional category is allowed in each geographical district. In practice, there is increasing union pluralism. Update: No substantial changes noted.
Chile	1996: The minimum number of workers required by law to establish an enterprise union, as well as the percentage it must represent in relation to the total of workers employed in the enterprise, make difficult the establishment in an enterprise of more than one union. Update: No substantial changes noted. [Per the US Department of State, the right to organise does not apply to police, military personnel and employees of state-owned companies attached to the Ministry of Defence.]

91

Table A.2. **Restrictions on the right to establish free unions**[a, b] *(cont.)*

China	1996: There is only one officially-recognised national union. The establishment of a union at the enterprise or professional level must be submitted for approval to the single existing union, which always denies it. Non-recognised unions are illegal; leaders of such unions have often been arrested.
	Update: No substantial changes noted. [Government submissions to the ILO appear to acknowledge that labour practices are in less than full conformity with ILO Convention 87, noting that trade unions must "abide by the constitution and law and dedicate themselves to the unity of the country and the nation."]
Chinese Taipei	1996: Authorities have discretionary power to certify a union. A non-certified union is disadvantaged in various ways (notably it cannot bargain collectively).
	Update: No substantial changes noted. [Teachers, civil servants and defence industry workers do not have the right to organise. Only one trade union confederation is permitted in each city, county or province.]
Colombia	1996: According to ILO, government officials can attend union meetings.
	Update: No substantial changes noted with respect to the above-mentioned issue. [In 1999, an observation of the CEACR stressed the "gravity" of the shortfalls in Colombian legislation with respect to ILO conventions including the limitation that only one union can register per workplace, the prohibition of strikes in a very wide range of public services which are not necessarily essential, and the power of the Minister of Labour to refer a dispute to arbitration when a strike lasts over a specific period, among other provisions.]
Ecuador	1996: According to ILO, the minimum number of workers required by law to establish an enterprise union is too high, making it difficult to establish unions in small enterprises.
	Update: No substantial changes noted. [The CEACR notes that new provisions in the 1998 Constitution may be interpreted as imposing a trade union monopoly in state institutions.]
Egypt	1996: There is only one legally-recognised union federation, which is closely related to the ruling party. Only one union per workplace is permitted. Authorities intervene in the election of union officers.
	Update: No substantial changes noted. [As a step toward conformity with Convention 87, the CEACR has urged the government to amend legal provisions that prohibit workers from establishing occupational organisations outside of the existing trade union structure.]
Ethiopia	1996: In 1993, the single union system, in vigour since 1975, was repealed.
	Update: The CEACR has expressed concern whether certain civil servants (*e.g.*, judges, prosecutors and others) in practise have the right to freely organise and promote their occupational interests. There are recent CFA cases involving interference with the right of freedom of association (nos. 1908 and 1888).
Fiji	1996: Until 1992, the only union federation was closely associated with the ruling party.
	Update: No substantial changes noted. [Employers are required to recognise a union if its membership includes over half of the employees in a workplace.]

Table A.2. **Restrictions on the right to establish free unions**[a, b] *(cont.)*

Guatemala	1996: According to ILO (Committee on Freedom of Association, case 1734), union rights are hampered by interference of employers associations in union activities in the food and beverages sector. Registration procedures are also long and bureaucratic.
	Update: The government has taken some steps to reduce the administrative impediments to trade union registration (*e.g.*, by reducing maximum processing time to 20 days from 60). However, at the same time, the CEACR recently repeated its comment that the government strictly supervises trade union activities.
Haiti	1996: Union rights have often been severely repressed.
	Update: No substantial changes noted. [The CEACR recently repeated its comment that Haiti requires government approval for workers to establish associations of more than 20 persons, that the government has wide powers to supervise trade unions, and that the law does not recognise the right of public servants to organise.]
Honduras	1996: Employers associations reportedly interfere in the functioning of unions (see CFA, case 1568). Only one union per workplace is permitted.
	Update: No substantial changes noted.
Hong Kong, China	1996: The right to form unions is recognised.
	Update: No substantial changes noted.
India	1996: Freedom of association is guaranteed. Enforcement is difficult in a few States, as registration of certain organisations is hampered by bureaucratic hurdles.
	Update: No substantial changes noted.
Indonesia	1996: Only recognised unions can bargain collectively and represent workers before the courts. To be recognised, a union must have offices in no less than 5 provinces, branch offices in no less than 27 districts. Plant-level units must exceed 100 in number. A union representing an industry located in a small geographical area must claim at least 10 000 members for it to be registered. Finally, labour authorities deny recognition to organisations that include lawyers, human rights activists or other so-called non-workers. There is a *de facto* union monopoly, as only one federation has been recognised, while new unions cannot obtain recognition unless they are affiliated to the single federation. The ruling party heavily interferes in the functioning of the single union federation. Most union leaders belong to the party.
	Update: Following Suharto's resignation in 1998, many of the barriers to establishment of free trade unions were eliminated (*e.g.*, the excessive numerical requirements). A new regulation, approved in June 1998, made possible the registration of some 20 new or previously unrecognised unions and thousands of workplace-level units. Several new trade union confederations have emerged. However, some unions have complained of difficulty in registering their workplace-level units.
Iran	1996: There is only one authorised labour organisation, which is close to the political regime.
	Update: No substantial changes noted.

93

Table A.2. **Restrictions on the right to establish free unions**[a, b] *(cont.)*

Israel	1996: Union rights are adequately protected. Palestinian workers cannot create a union whose aim would be to represent solely their interests but can affiliate freely to any other type of union.
	Update: No substantial changes noted.
Jamaica	1996: requirements consistent with ILO conventions.
	Update: No substantial changes noted.
Jordan	1996: The only existing union federation is heavily dependent of government financing.
	Update: No substantial changes noted. [Public servants do not have the right to organise.]
Kenya	1996: There is only one main union federation, which is subject to government interference. The government can arbitrarily de-register a union.
	Update: No substantial changes noted. [Except for civil servants, medical and university staff, most workers have the right to organise. In practise, workers in EPZs and small businesses may face dismissal for union activity with little effective recourse for reinstatement.]
Kuwait	1996: There is only one union federation. Foreigners can only join a union after five years of residence, subject to presentation of a certificate of good conduct, and can neither vote nor be elected. Unions cannot engage in any political or religious activity.
	Update: No significant changes noted.
Malaysia	1996: Authorities can deny legal existence to a union if it might be used "for unlawful purposes or other reasons". Appeal to an independent court is not possible in case of dissolution of a union. A union can only represent workers {in similar industries or professions}, so impeding the creation of nation-wide unions. {Additional requirements in effect prohibit formation of unions in the electronics industry.}
	Update: No substantial changes noted.
Malta	1996: requirements consistent with ILO conventions.
	Update: No substantial changes noted, however, the CEACR has pointed out certain discrepancies between Convention 87 and national legislation that gives the government powers to impose compulsory arbitration in a wide range of labour disputes.
Mauritius	1996: Authorities can arbitrarily de-register a union, and often do so in export processing zones.
	Update: The right to organise is laid out in the Constitution. The arbitrary de-registration of unions is no longer cited as a key problem (based on the sources for this table). EPZs are covered by national labour law, but in practise it is difficult for unions to organise there due to employer hostility and access restrictions.
Morocco	1996: Public authorities can limit union action because of political activity.
	Update: No substantial changes noted.

Table A.2. **Restrictions on the right to establish free unions**[a, b] *(cont.)*

Niger	1996: There is only one union federation, but others can be legally established. In practice the union federation is independent from political power. There are restrictions on the right to join unions for foreign workers.
	Update: The Constitution provides for the right to organise, but following the 1996 coup d'état police, water, customs, and forestry unions were abolished (per the US Department of State). Most union members are in the public sector. Also, there is now a small breakaway union confederation in addition to the main federation.
Pakistan	1996: Authorities can arbitrarily refuse registration of a union. Unions are banned in export processing zones. The Essential Services Act restricts trade union activity in certain firms.
	Update: No substantial changes noted.
Panama	1996: The minimum number of workers required by law to form a union is high. Authorities can inspect union activities. In export processing zones there are practically no unions.
	Update: A CEACR observation in 1999 commented that the minimum number of workers required by law to form a union remains too high (despite a reduction from 50 to 40 in 1995). The same observation noted restrictions on the number of public servants associations (one per institution and one chapter per province) were incompatible with the workers' right to freely choose their trade union.
Papua New Guinea	1996: requirements consistent with ILO conventions.
	Update: No substantial changes noted.
Peru	1996: The minimum number of workers required by law to form a union is high (100 workers).
	Update: No substantial changes noted.
Philippines	1996: For a union to be registered, its members must represent no less than a fifth of the workers of a bargaining unit. The law requires at least ten first-level unions to establish a federation. Update: No substantial changes noted with respect to the above-mentioned issues. [According to a 1998 ILO report, from the mid-1990s there has been a substantial improvement in industrial relations in public EPZs (*e.g.*, Bataan), while noting that anti-union policies persist in some private zones.]
Singapore	1996: Union registration is hampered by certain restrictions. Authorities have discretionary power to refuse registration. Nearly all union members belong to the National Trade Union, but workers seem to be satisfied with this situation, as in practice no other organisation has applied for registration status.
	Update: No substantial changes noted.
South Africa	1996: requirements consistent with ILO conventions.
	Updates: No substantial changes noted. [The Constitution (that came into effect in 1997) and the 1996 Labour Relations Act guarantee the right to organise for private sector and most public sector employees – only three security services are excluded. The law provides for a simplified trade union registration process.]

Table A.2. **Restrictions on the right to establish free unions**[a, b] (*cont.*)

Sri Lanka	1996: Unions must submit reports to labour authorities, otherwise they are de-registered.
	Update: No substantial changes noted. [Workers have the right to form trade unions and there are many operating. However, union organisers do not have access to EPZs and there are reportedly no unions functioning in these zones.]
Suriname	1996: requirements consistent with ILO conventions.
	Update: No substantial changes noted.
Swaziland	1996: According to the ILO, authorities interfere in unions' activities. Update: The 1996 Industrial relations Act limits the range of issues that can be addressed through union activity (*e.g.*, political or social issues cannot be addressed). Unions may not organise across industrial sectors.
Syria	1996: There is only one union federation, which is closely linked to the ruling party.
	Update: No substantial changes noted. [A series of decrees enforce a system of trade union unity. Also, the government has wide powers of intervention over trade union finances.]
Tanzania	1996: There is only one union federation, which is closely linked to the ruling party.
	Update: No substantial changes noted.
Thailand	1996: Freedom of association is warranted in the private sector. In 1991, the government dissolved state-enterprise unions. In these enterprises, the government can limit the number of unions, dissolve them and prevent affiliation with private sector unions. Most big companies belong to the State.
	Update: No substantial changes noted.
Uruguay	1996: requirements consistent with ILO conventions.
	Update: No substantial changes noted.
Venezuela	1996: The minimum number of workers required by law to form a union (of self-employed workers) is high (100 workers). According to the ILO, the list of attributions for workers organisations is too detailed. Foreign workers are eligible as union officers after 10 years of residence.
	Update: No substantial changes noted.
Zambia	1996: Only one union per (industry) is allowed.
	Update: No substantial changes noted. [Amendments in 1997 to the Industrial and Labour Relations Act removed impediments to the establishment of federations by trade unions (previously only the Zambia Congress of Labour was recognised).]
Zimbabwe	1996: Authorities can arbitrarily refuse registration and de-register existing unions.
	Update: No substantial changes noted. [Public servants may form associations, but not unions. Workers in EPZs are deprived of the right to freedom of association.]

Table A.2.   **Restrictions on the right to establish free unions**[a, b] *(cont.)*

OECD	
Australia	1996: requirements consistent with ILO conventions.
	Update: No substantial changes noted.
Austria	1996: requirements consistent with ILO conventions.
	Update: No substantial changes noted.
Belgium	1996: requirements consistent with ILO conventions.
	Update: No substantial changes noted.
Canada	1996: requirements consistent with ILO conventions.
	Update: No substantial changes noted. [There are however, several CFA cases (nos. 1951, 1975 and 1985) and CEACR comments concerning provincial restrictions on the right to organise or bargain collectively for specific occupations (*e.g.*, concerning certain hospital employees in Alberta or agricultural workers in Ontario) that appear to be inconsistent with Conventions 87 or 98.]
Czech Republic	1996: Not covered.
	Update: requirements consistent with ILO conventions.
Denmark	1996: The law is in agreement with ILO conventions. The law does not prohibit union security clauses.
	Update: No substantial changes noted.
Finland	1996: requirements consistent with ILO conventions.
	Update: No substantial changes noted.
France	1996: requirements consistent with ILO conventions.
	Update: No substantial changes noted.
Germany	1996: requirements consistent with ILO conventions.
	Update: No substantial changes noted.
Greece	1996: requirements consistent with ILO conventions.
	Update: No substantial changes noted.
Hungary	1996: Not covered.
	Update: requirements consistent with ILO conventions.
Iceland	1996: requirements consistent with ILO conventions.
	Update: No substantial changes noted.
Ireland	1996: requirements consistent with ILO conventions.
	Update: No substantial changes noted.
Italy	1996: requirements consistent with ILO conventions.
	Update: No substantial changes noted.
Japan	1996: requirements consistent with ILO conventions.
	Update: No substantial changes noted.

Table A.2.   **Restrictions on the right to establish free unions**[a, b] (*cont.*)

Korea	1996: The law permits only one union in each company. {…} Severe restrictions to the creation of federations and national confederations exist. Only one national confederation has been officially recognised so far.
	Update: New legislation in 1997 and an agreement in the Tripartite Commission in 1998 have improved the labour relations environment. Trade union pluralism is now permitted at the industrial and national levels and, from 2002, at enterprise level. In 1999, the formerly-dissident national trade union confederation (KCTU) and teachers trade union (Chonkyojo) were registered. Also, from 1999, many non-managerial public servants gained the right to form consultative employee associations (but not yet formal unions), although a number of employee categories are exempted from this provision such as public prosecutors, fire fighters and the police.
Luxembourg	1996: Not covered.
	Update: requirements consistent with ILO conventions.
Mexico	1996: There are no legal impediments to the formation of a union and the Mexican authorities state that registration is denied only when workers' organisations do not fulfil the administrative and procedural requirements established in the law. However, registration requirements are reportedly used to deny recognition to certain workers' organisations (US NAO, submission 3 (1995)). Most unions are affiliated to the Labour Congress (US State Department (1994)). Only one union can be formed in each government agency or state enterprise (ILO report of the Committee of Experts (1995)).
	Update: No substantial changes noted. [In 1999, the CEACR restated its concern with certain provisions in Mexican law that limit freedom of association, including those that prevent union members from quitting their unions, prohibit re-election of union officers, and limit rights of public servants to join unions, among other restrictions.]
Netherlands	1996: requirements consistent with ILO conventions.
	Update: No substantial changes noted.
New Zealand	1996: requirements consistent with ILO conventions.
	Update: No substantial changes noted.
Norway	1996: requirements consistent with ILO conventions.
	Update: No substantial changes noted.
Poland	1996: Not covered.
	Update: requirements consistent with ILO conventions.
Portugal	1996: requirements consistent with ILO conventions.
	Update: No substantial changes noted.
Spain	1996: requirements consistent with ILO conventions.
	Update: No substantial changes noted.
Sweden	1996: requirements consistent with ILO conventions.
	Update: No substantial changes noted.
Switzerland	1996: requirements consistent with ILO conventions.
	Update: No substantial changes noted.

Table A.2.   **Restrictions on the right to establish free unions**[a, b] *(cont.)*

Turkey	1996: In the present Constitution, several limitations to the right of free association remain (ILO (1994)). Government interferes in the functioning of unions, notably through the requirement that a government representative should attend unions' conventions (US State Department (1994)) .
	Update: Legal changes in the mid-1990s reduced limitations on the right of free association. Amendments to the Public Servants Act in 1997 specifically stated the right of public servants to form and join unions and upper-level union organisations. Also, per the Trade Unions Act (No. 2821), general congresses of unions and their confederations may open even if the government representative is not present. However, the CEACR (1999) has noted remaining areas of concern including the restriction that union officers may not be candidates for local administrative or general parliamentary elections and limitations on industrial action that are at variance with Convention 87.
United Kingdom	1996: requirements consistent with ILO conventions.
	Update: No substantial changes noted.
United States	1996: requirements consistent with ILO conventions. {A CFA case in 1993 (No. 1523) resulted in the recommendation that union representatives be guaranteed access to workplaces for purposes of informing and potentially organising workers.}
	Update: No substantial changes noted.

a) Abbreviations often used in Tables A.2-A.4 include:
   CEACR: The ILO's Committee of Experts on the Application of Conventions and Recommendations.
   CFA: The ILO's Committee on Freedom of Association.
b) The entries for Tables A.2-A.4 reflect information from sources available as of end-1999. Cases where the 1996 entry remained valid, but new or additional information of particular relevance was confirmed in 1999, are shown in square brackets [ ]. Corrections and additions to the actual 1996 entries are shown in curved brackets { }.
Source: ILO (1999*b*) and ILO (1999*f*) are the principle sources for the update entries; other sources for the update and 1996 entries include ICFTU (1999*a*), ILO (1998*b*), ILO (1998-9*d*), ILO (1999*e*), OECD (1996*b*), United States Department of State (1994 and 1999).

Table A.3. **Restrictions on the right to strike**

Non-OECD	
Argentina	1996: Organisations other than the one with representative status do not have the right to either call a strike or intervene in disputes.
	Update: Workers have the right to strike and it appears to be observed in practise.
Bahamas	1996: Prior administrative authorisation is needed for a strike to be legal.
	Update: No substantial changes noted.
Bangladesh	1996: Strikes are banned in sectors believed to be essential by the authorities.
	Update: Strikes are a common form of protest, but the right to strike is apparently not specifically protected in law. The Government continues to be able to bar strikes in key sectors under the Essential Services Ordinance.
Barbados	1996: No noticeable restrictions.
	Update: No substantial changes noted.
Bolivia	1996: General strikes and solidarity strikes are illegal.
	Update: Private sector workers have the right to strike subject to certain restrictions: a majority of ¾ of all workers in an enterprise is required to call a strike; general strikes and sympathy strikes are illegal; bank workers do not have the right to strike; and the government may impose compulsory arbitration to end a strike.
Botswana	1996: The right to strike is restricted by the imposition of compulsory arbitration.
	Update: No substantial changes noted.
Brazil	1996: Arbitration is compulsory in certain sectors.
	Update: No substantial changes noted.
Chile	1996: No noticeable restrictions.
	Update: No substantial changes noted. [Employees of essential services are apparently prohibited from striking.]
China	1996: The right to strike is not recognised.
	Update: No substantial changes noted. [In practise, strikes do occur and may be increasing in frequency. Several sources note allegations of repression of strikes.]
Chinese Taipei	1996: To be legal, strikes have to be approved by a majority of unionised workers. Authorities may impose mediation or arbitration procedures, during which a strike is illegal.
	Update: No substantial changes noted.
Colombia	1996: The right to strike is restricted by compulsory arbitration and the broad definition of essential services (where strikes are prohibited).
	Update: No substantial changes noted.
Ecuador	1996: Compulsory arbitration is possible.
	Update: The CEACR notes that the 1998 Constitution recognises and guarantees the right to strike, but excludes broadly defined essential services (*e.g.*, education)

Table A.3. **Restrictions on the right to strike** (*cont.*)

Egypt	1996: Strikes are practically illegal.
	Update: No substantial changes noted. [Although there is no legal right to strike, strikes do take place.]
Ethiopia	1996: Strikes are restricted by compulsory arbitration and lengthy notice periods. Update: No substantial changes noted. [Strikes are banned in a broad range of "essential services" (*e.g.*, banks).]
Fiji	1996: Strikes are subject to serious limitations.
	Update: recent legal changes mean that strike ballots can now be conducted without government supervision, but are still subject to government notification requirements.
Guatemala	1996: Cumbersome legal procedures make strikes difficult.
	Update: No substantial changes noted. [The CEACR recently repeated its observation that strike declarations require a ⅔ majority of workers in an enterprise.]
Haiti	1996: The duration of strikes is limited.
	Update: No substantial changes noted.
Honduras	1996: Strikes are subject to certain restrictions.
	Update: No substantial changes noted. [Civil servants do not have the right to strike. The CEACR recently repeated its observation that the restrictions on the right to strike include, among others, the requirement that ⅔ of the trade union membership are needed to call a strike and the power of the Minister of Labour and Social Security to suspend or pre-empt strikes in key sectors by requiring compulsory arbitration.]
Hong Kong, China	1996: Employment contracts can contain a clause whereby absences from work can lead to summary dismissal. Workers on strike can be dismissed under such a clause. Industrial actions are subject to legal intervention on criminal grounds, when action is believed to intimidate persons. These acts are punishable as criminal offences with fines or even imprisonment.
	Update: No substantial changes noted.
India	1996: Strikes are legally protected. Some restrictions apply in several states: authorities can prohibit strikes in essential services, defined in a relatively wide sense; mediation and arbitration procedures can be made mandatory in "essential industries".
	Update: No substantial changes noted. [Public sector unions are subject to advance notification requirements.]
Indonesia	1996: Mediation and prior notification to labour authorities is required for a strike to be declared legal. Because of difficulties in complying with these requirements, most strikes are illegal. Leaders of illegal strikes are often arrested.
	Update: No substantial changes noted.
Iran	1996: Strikes are strictly controlled.
	Update: No substantial changes noted.
Israel	1996: No noticeable restrictions.
	Update: No substantial changes noted.

Table A.3.   **Restrictions on the right to strike** (*cont.*)

Jamaica	1996: Employers are allowed to dismiss strikers. Essential services, where strikes are subject to severe limitations, are broadly defined. Update: No substantial changes noted. [The CEACR has observed that the Government's power to refer labour disputes for compulsory arbitration is too broad and should be limited through legal amendments.]
Jordan	1996: Authorities can declare a strike illegal by asking compulsory arbitration. Update: No substantial changes noted. [Workers must seek government permission to strike.]
Kenya	1996: Strikes are subject to lengthy notice periods and can be made illegal by the imposition of compulsory arbitration. Update: No substantial changes noted.
Kuwait	1996: Not covered. Update: There is no right to strike. Where negotiations fail, labour disputes are subject to compulsory arbitration.
Malaysia	1996: The right to strike is severely restricted by the practice of compulsory arbitration. For a strike to be legal, prior notification that proves the existence of a dispute must be given, and labour authorities can bring the dispute to the court. In the latter case, strikes cannot take place (legally) before the dispute is settled by the court. There are restrictions in "essential services", which include a comprehensive range of sectors. Strikes that pursue political ends or are called in sympathy with other striking workers are illegal. Update: No substantial changes noted. [Strikes are prohibited on a range of employment matters including wrongful dismissals.]
Malta	1996: Compulsory arbitration is possible. Update: No substantial changes noted. [See entry to Table A.2.]
Mauritius	1996: The right to strike is severely restricted by the imposition of long cooling-off periods. Compulsory arbitration is possible. Update: No substantial changes noted.
Morocco	1996: Strikes based on extra-professional motives are illegal. Offence to the freedom to work can be condemned by employers or authorities. Most strikes do not comply with conciliation procedures (which are very long) {…}. Update: No substantial changes noted.
Niger	1996: Conciliation is mandatory before strikes. Update: No substantial changes noted with respect to the above-mentioned issue. However, a government order in 1996 gave the government the power to requisition all state employees "in exceptional cases in order to preserve the general interest" including during strikes. The CEACR views this order as being too broad and going beyond essential services in the strict sense of the term.
Pakistan	1996: A strike believed to be against national interests can be prohibited and long cooling-off periods imposed. Update: No substantial changes noted.

Table A.3. **Restrictions on the right to strike** (*cont.*)

Panama	1996: No noticeable restrictions.
	Update: In 1997, new restrictions were imposed on industrial actions in EPZs requiring a period of 36 workdays of conciliation before a strike could be considered legal.
Papua New Guinea	1996: No noticeable restrictions.
	Update: No substantial changes noted.
Peru	1996: The government can suspend strikes.
	Update: No substantial changes noted. [A strike action must be endorsed by a majority of all workers in the workplace.]
Philippines	1996: For a strike to be legal, a majority of workers have to approve it, prior notice must be given and a "cooling-off" period observed. Labour authorities can prohibit strikes in "strategic industries" (defined in a wide sense). Illegal strikes give rise to fines and legal prosecution.
	Update: No substantial changes noted. [The CEACR has observed that the government has broad powers to impose compulsory arbitration to settle labour disputes to avoid strikes in any industry "indispensable to the national interest". It noted that this goes well beyond the scope permitted under Convention 87.]
Singapore	1996: Most disputes are settled through consultation with labour authorities. Strikes, though permitted by the law, are unusual.
	Update: No substantial changes noted.
South Africa	1996: A limit is imposed to the duration of strikes. Essential services are broadly defined.
	Update: Under the Constitution (that came into effect in 1997) and the Labour Relations Act of 1996, the right to strike has been guaranteed for most workers – excluding certain essential and security services. Labour disputes are first referred for conciliation. If conciliation fails to resolve the dispute, then a trade union may notify the employer of an intent to strike. Strikes conducted according to established procedures are not liable to criminal or civil action. Employers are permitted to hire replacement workers in place of striking employees (subject to 7 days' notice to the trade union).
Sri Lanka	1996: Strikes in essential services, broadly defined, are illegal.
	Update: No substantial changes noted. [Civil servants do not have the right to strike, although there have been recent instances where they have taken industrial actions.]
Suriname	1996: No noticeable restrictions.
	Update: No substantial changes noted.
Swaziland	1996: Strikes are subject to long mediation procedures.
	Update: No substantial changes noted. [The CEACR has noted that certain provisions in law aimed at limiting disturbances of the peace have been used to suppress strike action. Strikes are not permitted in a broad range of essential services (*e.g.*, including broadcasting).]
Syria	1996: There is no effective legal protection against anti-strike behaviour.
	Updates: No substantial changes noted. [Strikes are prohibited in the agricultural sector. Organisation of strikes is prohibited in a broad list of essential services.]

Table A.3.   **Restrictions on the right to strike** (*cont.*)

Tanzania	1996: Strikes are allowed only after complicated mediation and conciliation procedures. Update: No substantial changes noted.
Thailand	1996: Authorities can prohibit a strike in the private sector. In state enterprises the right to strike is not legally recognised. Update: No substantial changes noted. [Strikes are prohibited in essential services, which appear to be broadly defined.]
Uruguay	1996: No noticeable restrictions. Update: No substantial changes noted.
Venezuela	1996: No noticeable restrictions. Update: No substantial changes noted.
Zambia	1996: Strikes are subject to long cooling-off and conciliation periods. Update: No substantial changes noted.
Zimbabwe	1996: Strikes are subject to long cooling-off periods, and are forbidden in essential services, which are broadly defined. Update: No substantial changes noted. [Trade unions must provide the government with two weeks notice before any strike.]
OECD	
Australia	1996: No noticeable restrictions. Update: The Federal Workplace Relations Act of 1996 introduced a prohibition on certain strike actions (*e.g.*, during the period of operation of a collective agreement established under the act). The law clarifies that in certain circumstances, industrial actions are protected from civil liability; where these are not protected, such actions can result in injunctions and civil liabilities. As a result, the CEACR commented in 1999 that the effect is to excessively limit the subject matter of strikes, a point that remains under discussion with the government.
Austria	1996: No noticeable restrictions. Update: No substantial changes noted.
Belgium	1996: No noticeable restrictions. Update: No substantial changes noted.
Canada	1996: No noticeable restrictions Update: No substantial changes noted.
Czech Republic	1996: Not covered. Update: The right to strike is recognised except for those workers whose role in public order or public safety is deemed crucial.
Denmark	1996: No noticeable restrictions Update: No substantial changes noted.

Table A.3. **Restrictions on the right to strike** (*cont.*)

Finland	1996: No noticeable restrictions. Update: No substantial changes noted.
France	1996: No noticeable restrictions. Updates: No substantial changes noted.
Germany	1996: No noticeable restrictions. Updates: No substantial changes noted. |Civil servants do not enjoy the right to strike regardless of their function, a broad restriction that has been criticised by the ILO's CEACR.|
Greece	1996: No noticeable restrictions. Update: No substantial changes noted. |However, some legal restrictions on strikes appear to exist including a mandatory period of notice of four days for public utilities and 24 hours for the private sector. Legislation requires that a skeleton staff be maintained during strikes affecting public services.|
Hungary	1996: Not covered. Update: The right to strike is recognised except for military personnel and police officers.
Iceland	1996: No noticeable restrictions. Update: No substantial changes noted.
Ireland	1996: No noticeable restrictions. Update: No substantial changes noted.
Italy	1996: No noticeable restrictions. Update: No substantial changes noted.
Japan	1996: No noticeable restrictions. Update: No substantial changes noted. |Strikes by public servants are prohibited. A recent CEACR comment (CEACR, 1999) notes that the government should ensure adequate guarantees are provided to protect workers denied the right to strike. In a CFA case (1897) it was noted that such guarantees might include "adequate, impartial and speedy conciliation and arbitration procedures."|
Korea	1996: The law prohibits third-party intervention in labour disputes. In practice, independent unions (non-recognised) are often denied the right to intervene in disputes. In cases of non-respect, which occur frequently, strikers are laid off and union leaders arrested. The right to strike is subject to prior notification requirements and the imposition of 10-days "cooling-off" periods. In defence industries, the right to strike is prohibited. Update: Recent legal changes now permit third party intervention. Strikes remain prohibited for workers in local and central government and in enterprises that mainly produce military equipment. The right to strike remains restricted for employees in essential services where labour disputes are potentially subject to compulsory arbitration; these include rail and inner city bus services, utilities, and oil refinery and supply, hospital, banking and telecommunications services. Inner city buses and banking will no longer be considered essential services after 2000. The requirements for strike notification and cooling-off periods are still in effect.

105|

Table A.3. **Restrictions on the right to strike** (*cont.*)

Luxembourg	1996: Not covered.
	Update: The Constitution gives workers the right to strike, except for government workers providing essential services (such as police, armed forces and hospital personnel). However, in order for a strike to be legal, the Government's National Conciliation Office must certify that sufficient conciliation efforts were first undertaken. Strike leaders are protected by law against discrimination.
Mexico	1996: Conciliation by authorities is compulsory. Authorities consider this requirement guarantees the interests of workers. For a strike to be legal, certain conditions must be met. In particular, it must aim at harmonising the rights of labour and capital, it must be approved by a majority of workers and written notice must be given to the employer and labour authorities.
	Update: No substantial changes noted.
Netherlands	1996: No noticeable restrictions.
	Update: No substantial changes noted.
New Zealand	1996: Strikes are legal only in the context of the negotiation of a collective employment contract or safety and health issues and when they are not related to freedom of association, personal grievances and other disputes defined as disputes of rights (CFA, case No. 1678).
	Update: No substantial changes noted. [Current labour law limits the right to strike in cases where the aim is to force employers to become party to multi-company collective agreements.]
Norway	1996: Under certain circumstances, the government can invoke compulsory arbitration in labour disputes [CFA, case No. 1763 and cases therein].
	Update: No substantial changes noted.
Poland	1996: Not covered.
	Update: Unions have the right to strike except in "essential services". In order for a strike to be legal, apparently a cumbersome procedure must be followed. As a result, according to the US Department of State, many strikes are "technically" illegal.
Portugal	1996: No noticeable restrictions.
	Update: No substantial changes noted.
Spain	1996: No noticeable restrictions.
	Update: No substantial changes noted.
Sweden	1996: No noticeable restrictions.
	Update: No substantial changes noted.
Switzerland	1996: No noticeable restrictions.
	Update: No substantial changes noted. [The CEACR has commented (1999) that the 1927 law banning strike action by public servants is too broad, covering more than just those employees "exercising authority in the name of the state".]

Table A.3. **Restrictions on the right to strike** (*cont.*)

Turkey	1996: In mining, oil, defence and some other public services, workers do not have the right to strike. For a strike to be legal, prior collective bargaining and mediation is required. Authorities may suspend a strike for a 60-day period and ask for compulsory arbitration (ILO, report of the Committee of Experts (1994)). Workers in export processing zones do not have the right to strike for the first ten years of operation. During this period, disputes are settled by compulsory arbitration (US State Department (1994)).
	Update: No substantial changes noted. [Among the 9 EPZs, the suspension of the right to strike expired in 2 in 1997 and will expire in 2 more during 2000. In 1999, the CEACR requested that the government amend several pieces of legislation to bring them into conformity with Convention 87; these included sections concerning prohibition of protest and sympathy strikes, "severe limitations" on picketing, restriction of the right to strike for public employees in state enterprises and "severe sanctions, including imprisonment, for participation in 'unlawful' strikes not determined in accordance with freedom of association principles."]
United Kingdom	1996: Employers are allowed to dismiss strikers and selectively re-hire them after a period of three months (CFA, case No. 1540).
	Update: There is no specific statutory right to strike. The CEACR (1999) has expressed concern that legislation should provide strikers with adequate redress in the case of unfair disciplinary measures, particularly providing for reinstatement as an option in the case of dismissals. Strikers are not accorded immunities with respect to civil liabilities when undertaking sympathy strikes.
United States	1996: During strikes, employers can hire workers in replacement of strikers (CFA, case No. 1543).
	Update: No substantial changes noted.

Sources and notes: See Table A.2.

Table A.4. **Protection of union members and collective bargaining rights**

Non-OECD

Argentina	1996: Protection is adequate.
	Update: Argentine labour law prohibits anti-union practises and this is generally enforced by the government. There is an on-going freedom of association case (No. 1939) at the ILO involving several allegations of violations of union rights. Labour law reforms were passed in 1998 that (per the ICFTU) "confirmed the priority of industry-wide collective bargaining... and extended company-level collective agreements for a further year if agreement could not be reached by the parties on... re-negotiation."
Bahamas	1996: Protection is adequate.
	Update: No substantial changes noted.
Bangladesh	1996: Acts of anti-union discrimination are frequent and not adequately sanctioned. There is practically no collective bargaining in export processing zones and outside the organised sectors.
	Update: Violations continue. The CFA has noted (case No. 1862) several specific incidences and serious allegations concerning failure to register unions and anti-union discrimination against individuals.
Barbados	1996: Protection is adequate.
	Update: No substantial changes noted.
Bolivia	1996: Acts of anti-union discrimination are prohibited, but protection against such acts is inadequate owing to slow court proceedings.
	Update: No substantial changes noted. [The CEACR has noted that workers who are not trade union leaders suffer from a lack of protection against anti-union discrimination.]
Botswana	1996: Protection is adequate.
	Update: No substantial changes noted.
Brazil	1996: Anti-union legislation is not appropriately enforced. Unions estimate that cases of discrimination are seldom solved on time. Many of them take more than 5 years. Certain issues are excluded from collective bargaining.
	Update: No substantial changes noted.
Chile	1996: Protection is adequate.
	Update: No substantial changes noted.
China	1996: Collective bargaining is not possible in state-owned enterprises.
	Update: The 1995 national labour code in theory provides for collective bargaining, but this process appears to be seriously restricted. Government submissions to the ILO indicate that in 1997 collective agreements were concluded covering nearly 50 million workers.
Chinese Taipei	1996: Complicated mediation/arbitration procedures make collective bargaining difficult in small firms.
	Update: No substantial changes noted. [Penalties for anti-union discrimination appear to be inadequate.]

Table A.4. **Protection of union members and collective bargaining rights** (*cont.*)

Colombia	1996: There are ILO reports on grave acts of anti-union discrimination (CFA case No. 1686).
	Update: No substantial changes noted. [The CEACR comments that public employees "who are not engaged in the administration of the state" should be granted the right to bargain collectively. Colombian legislation does not conform to Convention 98 in this regard. The ILO and other sources cite numerous reports of violence against trade union officials.]
Ecuador	1996: Protection is adequate.
	Update: No substantial changes noted. [The CEACR has requested that the government "include in its legislation provisions which guarantee protection against acts of anti-union discrimination at the time of recruitment."]
Egypt	1996: There is practically no collective bargaining, as government sets {standards for} wages and working conditions by decree.
	Update: No substantial changes noted. [Private sector firms must adhere to certain government standards (*e.g.*, minimum wage), but have discretion in other non-binding areas such as bonuses.]
Ethiopia	1996: Protection is adequate.
	Update: No substantial changes noted. [However, there is an on-going CFA case (No. 1888) that appears to confirm serious cases of anti-union discrimination.]
Fiji	1996: Since 1992, free collective bargaining is permitted.
	Update: No substantial changes noted.
Guatemala	1996: Employment of union officers is not adequately protected.
	Update: No substantial changes noted. [There have been multiple cases of apparent anti-union discrimination. An on-going CFA case (No. 1970) documents a series of particularly serious incidences.]
Haiti	1996: Acts of anti-union discrimination have been numerous. There is virtually no collective bargaining.
	Update: No substantial changes noted.
Honduras	1996: Acts of anti-union discrimination are not adequately sanctioned. Blacklisting practices are reported in export processing zones.
	Update: No substantial changes noted.
Hong Kong, China	1996: A fine may be imposed in case a worker is prevented from joining a union, but reinstatement in the enterprise is not required by the law. However, the workers' right to join unions is legally established.
	Update: No substantial changes noted. [There are no laws stipulating collective bargaining and the government does not encourage it.]
India	1996: Protection is adequate.
	Update: No substantial changes noted.
Indonesia	1996: There is little effective protection against acts of anti-union discrimination.
	Update: No substantial changes noted. [Despite the improved environment following resignation of President Suharto, there remain cases of anti-union discrimination and interference. A recent CFA case (No. 1773) noted that further steps were required to ensure conformity with ILO conventions.]

Table A.4.   **Protection of union members and collective bargaining rights** (*cont.*)

Iran	1996: Little information is available on the right to organise and collective bargaining.
	Update: There is apparently little or no collective bargaining in practise.
Israel	1996: Protection is adequate.
	Update: No substantial changes noted.
Jamaica	1996: Though not prohibited, there are no unions in export processing zones. Possible anti-union practices in these zones are facilitated by the lack of inspections.
	Update: No substantive changes noted. [Also, the CEACR notes that collective bargaining rights may be denied in cases where no single union represents 40% of the workers or where the union fails to obtain support of 50% of all workers.]
Jordan	1996: Protection against acts of anti-union discrimination exists but is not adequately enforced.
	Update: No substantial changes noted.
Kenya	1996: Protection against acts of anti-union discrimination is reported to be inadequate.
	Update: No substantial changes noted.
Kuwait	1996: The situation is difficult to assess.
	Update: Reportedly, workers have the right to bargain collectively within certain limits (see Table A.3) and labour law prohibits anti-union discrimination.
Malaysia	1996: Anti-union discrimination is prohibited by law. But enforcement is weak due to long delays in court proceedings. Until 1993, collective bargaining rights were restricted in so-called "pioneer" industries.
	Update: The CEACR continues to object to the government's failure to reinstate full collective bargaining rights in companies granted "pioneer status".
Malta	1996: Protection is adequate.
	Update: No substantial changes noted.
Mauritius	1996: The government heavily interferes in collective bargaining.
	Update: A CEACR observation in 1998 highlighted the need to "adopt specific legal provisions in the near future to guarantee effective protection against acts of interference by employers and their organisations in the activities of workers' organisations, and *vice versa*, accompanied by effective and sufficiently dissuasive sanctions."
Morocco	1996: The ILO has registered complaints that certain union leaders have been arrested. Acts of anti-union discrimination are not adequately protected. Authorities may extend to other employers and workers a collective agreement to whom it did not originally apply. The initiative of extension often comes from the Minister of Labour and not from unions.
	Update: Apparently acts of anti-union discrimination continue (*e.g.*, CFA case No. 1877). The CEACR has also commented on the need to "promote development and utilisation of the machinery" for collective bargaining.
Niger	1996: Protection is adequate.
	Update: No substantive changes noted.

Table A.4. **Protection of union members and collective bargaining rights** (*cont.*)

Pakistan	1996: Acts of anti-union discrimination are not adequately sanctioned (CFA, cases No. 1771 and No. 1726).
	Update: Apparently, acts of anti-union discrimination continue (*e.g.*, see CFA case No. 1903). Although collective bargaining rights are available to legally-formed unions, there are restrictions on organisation that precludes collective bargaining rights for much of the labour force (*e.g.*, agricultural workers, workers in broadly defined essential services).
Panama	1996: Employment security of union officers is not adequate, especially in export processing zones.
	Update: The law provides most workers with the right to bargain collectively and protections against anti-union discrimination. However, the conclusions of a CFA case (No. 1931) noted that certain provisions in the labour code constitute undue interference and are contrary to collective bargaining principles (*e.g.*, by restricting the parties to the collective bargaining process).
Papua New Guinea	1996: Authorities can arbitrarily cancel a collective agreement.
	Update: No substantial changes noted. [Anti-union discrimination by employers is prohibited by law.]
Peru	1996: There are some limitations to collective bargaining.
	Update: No substantial changes noted. [However, it appears that there is insufficient protection for workers from anti-union discrimination (*e.g.*, at time of recruitment, in cases of wrongful dismissal where reinstatement might be an appropriate remedy or in cases where court decisions are too slow).]
Philippines	1996: Anti-union practices exist despite the fact that protective legislation is in place.
	Update: No substantial changes noted.
Singapore	1996: Annual wage supplements in new enterprises are limited. Promotion, dismissals, transfers and work organisation matters are excluded from the scope of collective bargaining. The court has discretionary powers to reject a collective agreement established in a new enterprise.
	Update: No substantial changes noted. [The law prohibits anti-union discrimination.]
South Africa	1996: Acts of anti-union discrimination are inadequately penalised in certain parts of the country.
	Update: The 1996 Labour Relations Act defines and protects the right to bargain collectively. The law removed administrative interference in the internal affairs of unions, provided protection against dismissal for strike action and enabled extension to third parties, of collective sectoral agreements concluded by bargaining councils. Workers are protected by law against anti-union discrimination.
Sri Lanka	1996: Workers in export processing zones cannot be represented by national unions.
	Update: Although workers in EPZs legally have the right to organise, in practise various barriers continue to prevent their organisation and representation by national unions. There are reports that in some instances laws are not effective in protecting workers from anti-union discrimination. Collective bargaining is widely practised outside of EPZs, but the law does not oblige employers to recognise and negotiate with trade unions.

111

Table A.4. **Protection of union members and collective bargaining rights** (*cont.*)

Suriname	1996: Protection is adequate. Update: No substantial changes noted.
Swaziland	1996: The Court may deny registration of a collective bargaining {agreement} if it does not comply with government directives. Update: No substantial changes noted. [There are legal provisions against anti-union discrimination. The CEACR notes that certain provisions of law could be used by government to suppress or interfere with legitimate trade union activity.]
Syria	1996: There is practically no collective bargaining. Update: No substantial changes noted.
Tanzania	1996: Collective agreements must be approved by the judiciary. Update: No substantial changes noted. [Collective bargaining takes place only in the private sector.]
Thailand	1996: Collective bargaining is severely restricted in state-enterprises. Update: No substantial changes noted. [Laws may not provide adequate protection against anti-union discrimination. The government sets wages for civil servants and employees in state sector enterprises.]
Uruguay	1996: Protection is adequate. Update: No substantial changes noted.
Venezuela	1996: Acts of anti-union discrimination are not adequately sanctioned (ILO, CFA, case 1739). Update: No substantial changes noted. [A trade union may only negotiate a collective agreement if it represents an absolute majority of the workers in an enterprise.]
Zambia	1996: Protection is adequate. Update: No substantial changes noted.
Zimbabwe	1996: The situation is difficult to assess. Update: Collective agreements must be registered and the government retains the right to veto agreements harmful to the economy. Employers are prohibited by law from anti-union discrimination. A CFA case (No. 1909) resulted in a reminder from the Committee to the government that it should respect the principles relating to the right to demonstrate of workers and noting that "depriving trade unionists of their freedom on grounds related to their trade union activity... constitute(s) an obstacle to the exercise of trade union rights." Per the ILO, workers in EPZs are denied the right to bargain collectively and are not protected against anti-union discrimination.
OECD	
Australia	1996: Protection is adequate. Update: The Workplace Relations Act of 1996 provides for collective bargaining and for negotiation of agreements between employers and individual workers. In 1998, the CEACR commented that certain provisions of the act "do not promote collective bargaining as required under Article 4 of the Convention", a point that remains under discussion with the government.

Table A.4. **Protection of union members and collective bargaining rights** (*cont.*)

Austria	1996: Protection is adequate. Update: No substantial changes noted.
Belgium	1996: Protection is adequate. Update: No substantial changes noted.
Canada	1998: Protection against acts of anti-union discrimination is adequate. According to ILO, restrictions apply in the public sector for certain Provinces. Update: No substantial changes noted.
Czech Republic	1996: Not covered. Update: Protection is adequate.
Denmark	1996: Protection is adequate. Update: No substantial changes noted.
Finland	1996: Protection is adequate. Update: No substantial changes noted.
France	1996: Protection is adequate. Update: No substantial changes noted.
Germany	1996: Protection is adequate. Update: No substantial changes noted.
Greece	1996: Protection is adequate. Update: No substantial changes noted.
Hungary	1996: Not covered. Update: Protection is adequate.
Iceland	1996: Protection is adequate. Update: No substantial changes noted.
Ireland	1996: Protection is adequate. Update: No substantial changes noted.
Italy	1996: Protection is adequate. Update: No substantial changes noted.
Japan	1996: Protection is adequate. Update: No substantial changes noted.
Korea	1996: Workers of unregistered federations and confederations do not have the right to intervene in company-level union activities, including collective bargaining (prohibition of third party intervention). Certain Members of unregistered unions have been subject to legal prosecution as a result of third party intervention. Update: Changes in labour law have largely removed the restrictions on third-party intervention in collective bargaining and labour disputes. [The right to bargain collectively is provided for by law. Workers are also legally protected against retribution for legal strike actions. At the same time, there have been numerous incidences of arrests of trade union members, generally for alleged violence or obstruction of business during labour disputes.]

113

Table A.4. **Protection of union members and collective bargaining rights** (*cont.*)

Luxembourg	1996: Not covered.
	Update: Protection is adequate.
Mexico	1996: The situation is difficult to assess.
	Update: Labour law protects labour organisations from interference in internal affairs and workers from anti-union discrimination. However, there are reports that with respect to the latter, enforcement may be uneven or inadequate in some areas.
Netherlands	1996: Protection is adequate.
	Update: No substantial changes noted.
New Zealand	1996: Protection against acts of anti-union discrimination is adequate. Legislation prohibits strikes designed to force an employer to enter multi-employer collective bargaining (ILO, CFA, case 1763). {The CFA noted (case No. 1698, dated 1994) that labour legislation did not conform with ILO principles, and specifically that it did not promote collective bargaining nor provide sufficient protection in certain cases of employer interference in union affairs.}
	Update: No substantial changes noted. [Current law provides for the right of workers to organise and bargain collectively (except members of the armed forces). Individual employees and employers may choose to negotiate agreements individually or collectively.]
Norway	1996: Protection is adequate.
	Update: No substantial changes noted.
Poland	1996: Not covered.
	Update: Legal protections against anti-union discrimination exist, but the CEACR has expressed concern that the penalties implied by the law are insufficient and are not an effective deterrent.
Portugal	1996: Protection is adequate.
	Update: No substantial changes noted.
Spain	1996: Protection is adequate.
	Update: No substantial changes noted.
Sweden	1996: Protection is adequate.
	Update: No substantial changes noted.
Switzerland	1996: Protection is adequate.
	Update: No substantial changes noted.
Turkey	1996: To have bargaining power in a particular enterprise, a union must represent the majority of the workers of that enterprise and 10% of the workers of the relevant industry (ILO, Committee of Experts (1994)).
	Update: No substantial changes noted. [The CEACR (2000) noted that the dual criteria for determining trade union representative status "do not appear to be observed by organisations of workers which, in practice, are free to pursue free collective bargaining". It asked the government to remove the restrictions formally and to grant collective bargaining rights to public servants. Also, it noted that Act No. 3218 provides for the use of compulsory arbitration under certain circumstances in EPZs and requested the government "take the necessary measures to ensure that all workers in all EPZs enjoy the right to negotiate freely…". Effective protection against anti-union discrimination, including provisions for reinstatement in cases of dismissal, is apparently not available to all workers.]

Table A.4. **Protection of union members and collective bargaining rights** (*cont.*)

United Kingdom	1996: ILO experts have in the past raised questions on the adequacy of application procedures, but these have now been answered.
	Update: The CEACR commented that there may be inadequate protection for striking workers singled-out for disciplinary action by employers and requested a strengthening of legislation protecting workers against anti-union discrimination. A recent CFA case (No. 1852) concluded with a recommendation that the government take steps to amend current labour legislation to ensure that workers' organisations have adequate protection from undue interference by employers and that collective bargaining is not discouraged.
United States	1996: Unions report that acts of anti-union discrimination are not adequately protected. A complaint whereby procedures to obtain compensation for illegal dismissal for reason of union activity are too slow was presented to the ILO (CFA, case No. 1543). {A further CFA case (No. 1557) resulted in the conclusion that there were possible instances of non-conformity with ILO Convention 98 with respect to certain restrictions on the rights for some state or local government employees to bargain collectively.}
	Update: No substantial changes noted.

Sources and notes: See Table A.2.

References

BASU, K. (1999),
"Child Labour: Cause, Consequence and Cure, with Remarks on International Labor Standards", *Journal of Economic Literature* XXXVII, September, pp. 1083-1119.

BASU, K. and VAN, P.H. (1998),
"The Economics of Child Labor", *The American Economic Review*, Vol. 88, No. 3, June.

BERMAN, E., MACHIN, S. and BOUND, J. (1996),
"Implications of Skill-Biased Technological Change: International Evidence", Boston University, December, mimeo.

BLANPAIN, R. and ENGELS, C. (1998),
European Labour Law, Kluwer Law International, The Hague.

BORJAS, G.J., FREEMAN, R.B. and KATZ, L.F. (1997),
"How much do Immigration and Trade Affect Labor Market Outcomes?", Brookings Paper on Economic Activity, No. 1, pp. 317-344.

BORJAS, G.J. and RAMEY, V. (1995),
"Foreign Competition, Market Power, and Wage Inequality", *Quarterly Journal of Economics* 110, No. 4, pp. 1075-1110, November.

BROWN, D.K. (1999),
"Can Consumer Product Labels Deter Foreign Child Labor Exploitation?", Working Paper No. 99-19, Department of Economics, Tufts University.

BROWN, D.K., DEARDORFF, A.V. and STERN, R.M. (1999),
"US Trade and Other Policy Options and Programs to Deter Foreign Exploitation of Child Labor", Discussion Paper 99-04, Department of Economics, Tufts University.

CASSELLA, A. (1996),
"Free Trade and Evolving Standards", in Jagdish Bhagwati and Robert Hudec (eds.), *Fair Trade and Harmonization: Prerequisites for Free Trade?*, Vol. 1 *Economic Analysis*, Cambridge University Press, Cambridge, MA.

CLINE, W.R. (1997),
Trade and Income Distribution, Institute for International Economics, Washington, DC.

CORDEN, W.M. and VOUSDEN, N. (1997),
"Paved with Good Intentions: Social Dumping and Raising Labour Standards in Developing Countries," School of Advanced International Studies, The Johns Hopkins University, manuscript.

DILLER, J. (2000),
"Social Conduct in transaction enterprises operations: the role of the International Labor Organization", in Roget Blanpain (ed.) *Multinational Enterprises and the Social Challenges of the XXIst Century, Bulletin of Comparative Labour Relations*, Vol. 37, pp. 17-28.

ELMSLIE, B. and MILBERG, W. (1996),
 "Free Trade and Social Dumping: Lessons from the Regulation of US Interstate Commerce", *Challenge*, May-June.

FELICIANO, Z. (1995),
 "Workers and Trade Liberalization: The Impact of Trade Reforms in Mexico on Wages and Employment", Queens College, New York, May, mimeo.

FINANCIAL TIMES (1999),
 "The Value of Virtue in a Transparent World", 5 August.

FREEMAN, R. (1993),
 "Labor Market Institutions and Policies: Help or Hindrance to Economic Development?", *Proceedings of the World Bank Annual Conference on Development Economics* 1992, World Bank, Washington, DC, pp. 117-144.

FREEMAN, R. (1996),
 "When Earnings Diverge: Causes, Consequences, and Cures for the New Inequality in the US", unpublished paper.

GORDON, K. and MIYAKE, M. (1999),
 "Deciphering Codes of Corporate Conduct", Working Papers on International Investment No. 99/2, November.

GOUX, D. and MAURIN, E. (1997),
 "The Decline in Demand for Unskilled Labour: An Empirical Analysis and the Application to France", INSEE, Paris, March, mimeo.

HARRISON, A. and LEAMER, E.E. (1997),
 "Labor Markets in Developing Countries: An Agenda for Research", *Journal of Labor Economics*.

ICFTU (1996),
 "Behind the wire: Anti-union repression in the Export Processing Zones", survey prepared for the ICFTU by Jean-Paul Marhoz with Marcela Szymanski, April.

ICFTU (1999a),
 Annual Survey of Violations of Trade Union Rights, various issues, International Confederation of Free Trade Unions, Internet posting (*http://www.icftu.org*).

ICFTU (1999b),
 Building Workers' Human Rights into the Global Trading System.

ILO (1994),
 ILOLEX: *the ILO's database on International Labour Standards*, International Labour Organisation, Geneva.

ILO (1998a),
 ILO *Declaration on Fundamental Principles and Rights at Work and Its Follow-Up*, International Labour Office, Geneva.

ILO (1998b),
 Labour and social issues relating to export processing zones, International Labour Office, Geneva.

ILO (1998c),
 "Report for discussion at the Tripartite Meeting of Export Processing Zones-Operating Countries", International Labour Office, Geneva.

ILO (1998-9d),
Country Studies on the Social Impact of Globalisation, Task Force on Country Studies on Globalisation, International Labour Office, Geneva, various country studies.

ILO (1999a),
Handbook of procedures relating to international labour Conventions and Recommendations, International Labour Standards Department, International Labour Office, rev.2/1998, Internet posting (http://www.ilo.org/public/english/standards/norm/sources/handbook/index.htm), 30 November, Geneva.

ILO (1999b),
ILOLEX: the ILO's database on International Labour Standards, International Labour Organisation, Internet posting (http://ilolex.ilo.ch:1567/public/english/50normes/infleg/iloeng/iloquery.htm), various dates (December 1999- June 2000) and CD Rom (1999 edition).

ILO (1999c),
"IPEC action against child labour, achievements, lessons learned and indications for the future", International Labour Organisation, Geneva.

ILO (1999d),
Programme and Budget Proposals for 2000-01: Introductory Statement by the Director-General, GB/274/PFA/9/3, Governing Body, International Labour Office, March.

ILO (1999e),
Ratification and promotion of fundamental ILO Conventions, GB.276/LILS/6, International Labour Office, Governing Body, November, Internet posting (http://www.ilo.org/public/english/standards/relm/gb/docs/gb276/lils-6.htm).

ILO (1999f),
Report of the Committee of Experts on the Application of Conventions and Recommendations: general report and observations concerning particular countries, report III (Part 1A), International Labour Office, Geneva.

ILO (2000a),
Review of Annual Reports Under the Follow-Up to the ILO Declaration on Fundamental Principles and Rights at Work, Parts I and II, International Labour Office, Geneva, March.

ILO (2000b),
Your Voice at Work: Global Report Under the Follow-Up to the ILO Declaration on Fundamental Principles and Rights at Work, International Labour Office, Geneva.

JESSUP, D. (1999),
"Dollars and Democracy: Developing Country Democracies' Declining Share of Trade and Investment Markets", New Economy Information Services, November 10.

KRUEGER, A.B. (1996),
"Observations on International Labor Standards and Trade", National Bureau of Economic Research Working Paper No. 5632.

KRUGMAN, P. (1995),
"Technology, Trade, and Factor Prices", National Bureau of Economic Research (NBER) Working Paper No. 5355.

KURUVILLA, S. (1996),
"Linkages between Industrialization Strategies and Industrial Relations/Human Resource Policies: Singapore, Malaysia, the Philippines, and India", Industrial and Labor Relations Review 49, No. 4.

LAWRENCE, R.Z. (1996),
> *Single World Divided Nations? International Trade and OECD Labour Markets*, OECD Development Centre, Paris.

LEVINSOHN, J. (1996),
> "Competition Policy and International Trade Policy", in J. Bhagwati and R. Hudec (eds.) *Fair Trade and Harmonization: Prerequisites for Free Trade?*, Vol. 1, *Economic Analysis*, Cambridge University Press, Cambridge, MA.

MAH, J.S. (1997),
> "Core Labour Standards and Export Performance in Developing Countries." *World Economy* 20, No. 6, pp. 773-785, September.

MASKUS, K. (1997),
> "Should Core Labor Standards be Imposed Through International Trade Policy?", World Bank Policy Research Working Paper No. 1817, August.

MEXICO, Secretaria De Desarrollo Social (1998),
> "Mexico's New Social Policy", paper prepared for OECD meeting at Ministerial level on Social Policy, Paris, 23-24 June.

NEVEN, D. and WYPLOSZ, C. (1996),
> "Relative Prices, Trade and Restructuring in European Industry", Centre for Economic Policy Research Working Paper No. 1451, August.

OECD (1994),
> *Employment Outlook*, Paris.

OECD (1996a),
> *Shaping the 21st Century: The Contribution of Development co-operation A Development Partnership Strategy*, Development Assistance Committee, Paris.

OECD (1996b),
> *Trade, Employment and Labour Standards: A Study of Core workers' Rights and International Trade* Paris.

OECD (1997),
> *Employment Outlook*, Paris.

OECD (1998a),
> *Open Markets Matter: The Benefits of Trade and Investment Liberalisation*, Paris.

OECD (1998b),
> *Strengthening development partnerships: A working checklist*, Development Assistance Committee, Paris.

OECD (1999),
> "Codes of Corporate Conduct: An Inventory", report prepared for the Working Party of the Trade Committee [TD/TC/WP(98)74/FINAL], Paris.

OMAN, C. (2000),
> *Policy Competition for Foreign Direct Investment: A Study of Competition Among Governments to Attract FDI*, OECD Development Centre Studies, Paris.

PALLEY, T.I. (1999),
> "The Economic Case for International Labor Standards: Theory and Some Evidence", mimeo, AFL-CIO, Washington, DC.

PATRINOS, H.A. and PSACHAROPOULOS, G. (1997),
> "Family Size, Schooling and Child Labor in Peru", *Journal of Population Economics* 10, No. 4.

ROBBINS, D.J. (1996),
  "Evidence on Trade and Wages in the Developing World", OECD Development Centre Technical Papers, No. 119, December.

RODRIK, D. (1996),
  "Labor Standards in International Trade: Do They Matter and What Do We Do About Them", in R.Z. Lawrence, D. Rodrik and J. Whalley (eds.) Emerging Agenda For Global Trade: High Stakes for Developing Countries, Overseas Development Council Essay No. 20, Johns Hopkins University Press Washington, DC.

RODRIK, D. (1997a),
  "Democracy and Economic Performance", manuscript.

RODRIK, D. (1997b),
  Has Globalization Gone Too Far?, Institute for International Economics, Washington, DC.

ROGERS, C.A. and SWINNERTON, K.A. (2000),
  "Inequality, Productivity and Child Labor: Theory and Evidence", February.

ROMERO, A.T. (1995),
  "Labour Standards and Export Processing Zones: Situation and Pressures for Change", Development Policy Review 13, pp. 247-276.

STIGLITZ, J. (2000),
  "Democratic Development as the Fruits of Labor", Keynote Address, Industrial Relations Research Association, Boston, January.

SRINIVASAN, T.N. (1996),
  "International Trade and Labor Standards from an Economic Perspective", in Pitou van Dijck and Gerrit Faber (eds.), Challenges in the New World Trade Organization, Kluwer Law International, Amsterdam, pp. 219-243.

SWINNERTON, K.A. and ROGERS, C.A. (1999),
  "The Economics of Child Labour: Comment", American Economic Review 89(5), December, pp. 1382-85.

UN (1999),
  Treaty Bodies Database, United Nations High Commissioner for Human Rights, Internet posting (http://www.unhchr.ch/tbs/doc.nsf), various dates.

UNCTAD (1999a),
  Handbook of International Trade and Development Statistics: 1996/1997, United Nations Conference on Trade and Development, New York and Geneva.

UNCTAD (1999b),
  World Investment Report, 1999.

UNICEF (1994),
  Children at Work, UNICEF East Asia and Pacific Regional Office, Bangkok.

UNICEF (1997),
  State of the World's Children 1997.

UNITED STATES DEPARTMENT OF STATE (1994),
  Country Reports on Human Rights Practices for 1993, Washington, DC.

UNITED STATES DEPARTMENT OF STATE (1999),
  Country Reports on Human Rights Practices for 1998, Washington, DC, February.

USDOL (1996),

> *The Apparel Industry and Codes of Conduct: A Solution to the International Child Labor Problem?*
> US Department of Labor, Washington, DC, available as an Internet posting (*http://www.dol.gov/dol/ilab/public/media/reports/iclp/apparel/main.htm*).

USDOL (1998),

> *By the Sweat and Toil of Children (Volume 5): Efforts to Eliminate Child Labour*, US Department of Labor, Washington, DC, available as an Internet posting (*http://www.dol.gov/dol/ilab/public/media/reports/iclp/sweat5/*).

VAN BEERS, C. (1998),

> "Labour Standards and Trade Flows of OECD Countries", *World Economy* 21, No. 1, pp. 57-73, January.

WILSON, J.D. (1996),

> "Capital mobility and environmental standards: is there a theoretical basis for a race to the bottom?", in Jagdish Bhagwati and Robert Hudec (eds.), *Fair Trade and Harmonization Prerequisites for Free Trade?*, Vol. 1 *Economic Analysis*, MIT Press, Cambridge and London, pp. 393-427.

WORLD BANK (1995),

> *Workers in an Integrating World: World Development Report*, Oxford University Press, Oxford and New York.

WORLD BANK (1998),

> *Child labour: Issues and Directions for the World Bank.*

WTO (1996),

> *Singapore Ministerial Declaration*, adopted on 13 December 1996 at the Ministerial Conference of the, World Trade Organisation, Internet posting (*http://www.wto.org/wto/ddf/ep.public.html*, document symbol WT/MIN(96)/DEC).

WTO (1999a),

> "Proposal for a Joint ILO/WTO Standing Working Forum on Trade, Globalization and Labour Issues", WT/GC/W/383, 5 November.

WTO (1999b),

> "WTO's forward Work Programme: Proposed Establishment of a Working Group on Trade and Labour", WT/GC/W/382, 1 November.

WTO (1999c),

> "The WTO and International Economic Policy Coherence", WT/GC/W/360, 12 October.